For Engineers & Designers

T-FLEX CAD Exercises

200 3D PRACTICE DRAWINGS

SACHIDANAND JHA

cadin360°
Learning Tutorials

Dear Reader,

Thank you for choosing **T-FLEX CAD Exercises** book. This book is part of a family of premium-quality CADIN360 books, all of which are written by Outstanding author who combine practical experience with a gift for teaching.

CADIN360 was founded in 2016. More than 3 years later, we're still committed to producing consistently exceptional books. With each of our titles, we're working hard to set a new standard for the industry. From the paper we print on, to the authors we work with, our goal is to bring you the best books available.

I hope you see all that reflected in these pages. I'd be very interested to hear your comments and get your feedback on how we're doing. Feel free to let me know what you think about this or any other CADIN360 book by sending me an email at contactus@cadin360.com.

If you think you've found a technical error in this book, please visit
https://cadin360.com/contact-us/.
Customer feedback is critical to our efforts at CADIN360.

Best regards,

Sachidanand Jha
Founder & CEO, CADIN360

T-FLEX CAD Exercises

Published by
CADIN360
cadin360.com
Copyright © 2019 by CADIN360, All rights reserved.

Preface

T-FLEX CAD Exercises

❖ This book contain 200 CAD practice exercises and drawings.

❖ This book does not provide step by step tutorial to design 3D models.

❖ S.I Unit is used.

❖ Predominantly used Third Angle Projection.

❖ This book is for **T-FLEX CAD** and Other Feature-Based Modeling Software such as Inventor, SolidWorks, NX, Solid Edge, AutoCAD, PTC Creo etc.

❖ It is intended to provide Drafters, Designers and Engineers with enough 3D CAD exercises for practice on **T-FLEX CAD**.

❖ It includes almost all types of exercises that are necessary to provide, clear, concise and systematic information required on industrial machine part drawings.

❖ Third Angle Projection is intentionally used to familiarize Drafters, Designers and Engineers in Third Angle Projection to meet the expectation of world wide Engineering drawing print.

❖ Clear and well drafted drawing help easy understanding of the design.

❖ This book is for Beginner, Intermediate and Advance CAD users.

❖ These exercises are from Basics to Advance level.

❖ Each exercises can be assigned and designed separately.

❖ No Exercise is a prerequisite for another. All dimensions are in mm.

❖ Note: Assume any missing dimensions.

EX-01

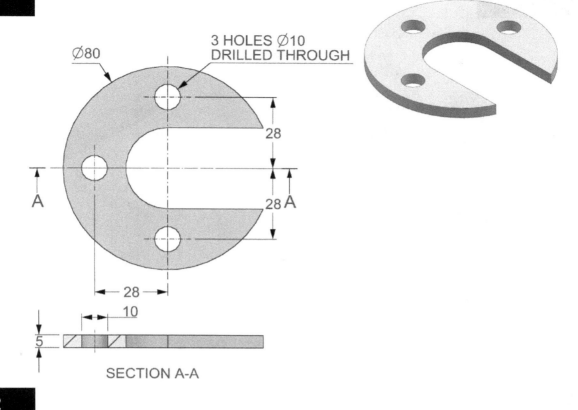

Ø80

3 HOLES Ø10
DRILLED THROUGH

28

28 A

A

28

10

5

SECTION A-A

EX-02

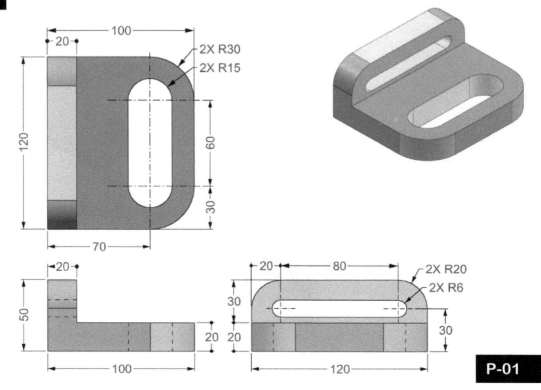

100

20

2X R30

2X R15

120

60

30

70

20

50

20

20

100

20   80

2X R20

2X R6

30

30

120

P-01

EX-03

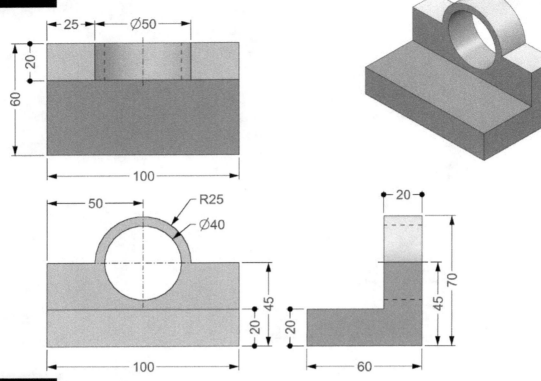

25 · Ø50 · 20 · 60 · 100

50 · R25 · Ø40 · 45 · 20 · 20 · 100 · 20 · 70 · 45 · 60

EX-04

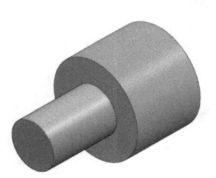

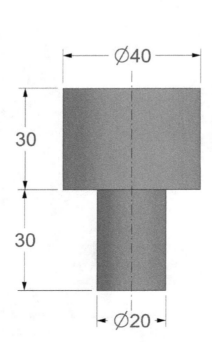

Ø40 · 30 · 30 · Ø20

P-02

EX-05

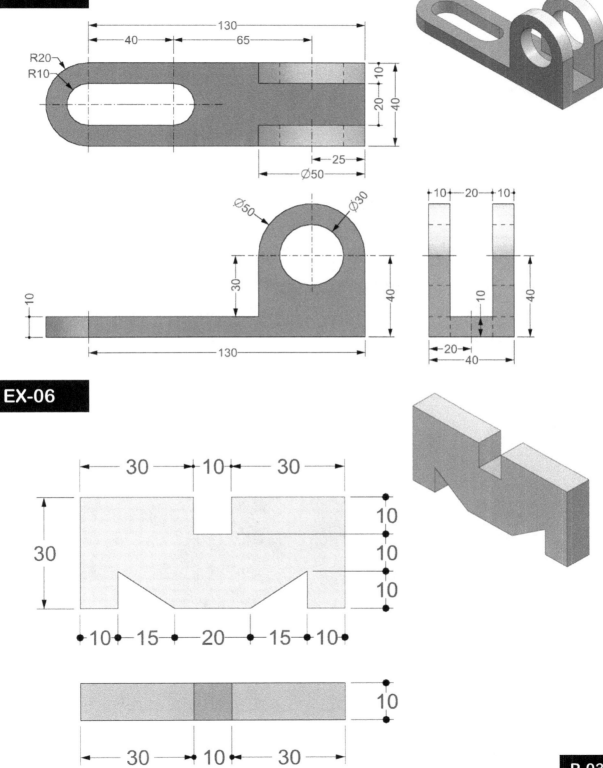

EX-06

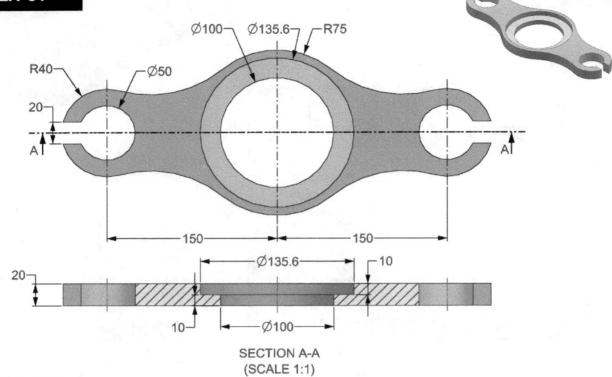

Ø100 Ø135.6 R75

R40 Ø50

20

A

150 150

20

Ø135.6 10

10 Ø100

SECTION A-A
(SCALE 1:1)

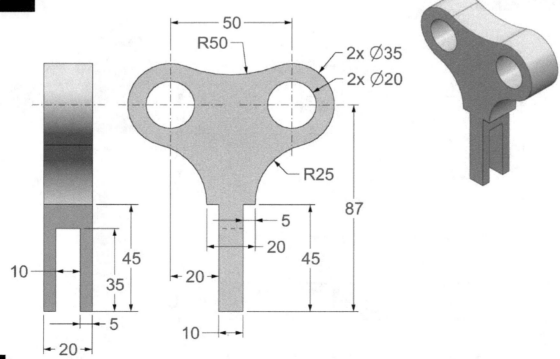

50

R50

2x Ø35

2x Ø20

R25

87

5

20

45

45

20

10 10

20

35

5

20

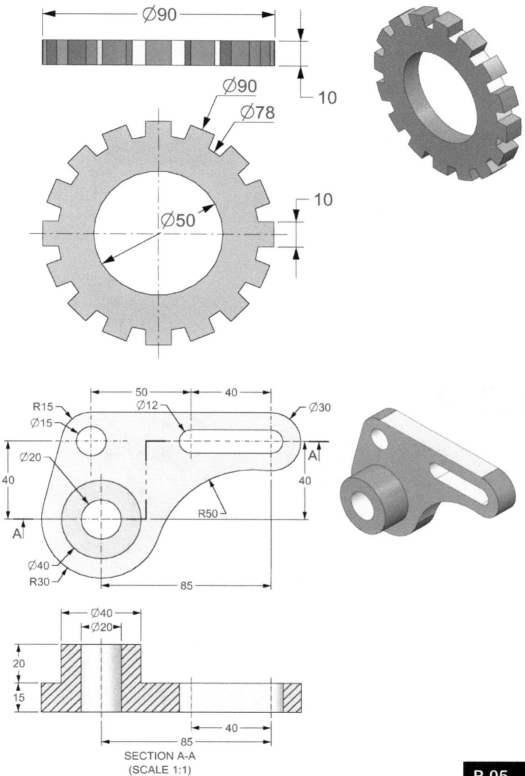

EX-09

⌀90

10

⌀90
⌀78
⌀50
10

EX-10

50
40
R15
⌀15
⌀12
⌀30
⌀20
A
40
40
R50
A
R30
⌀40
85

⌀40
⌀20
20
15
40
85
SECTION A-A
(SCALE 1:1)

P-05

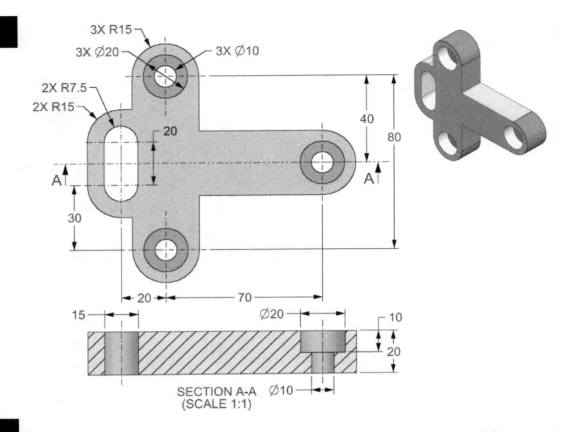

3X R15
3X Ø20
3X Ø10
2X R7.5
2X R15
20
40
80
A
30
20
70

15
Ø20
10
20
Ø10

SECTION A-A
(SCALE 1:1)

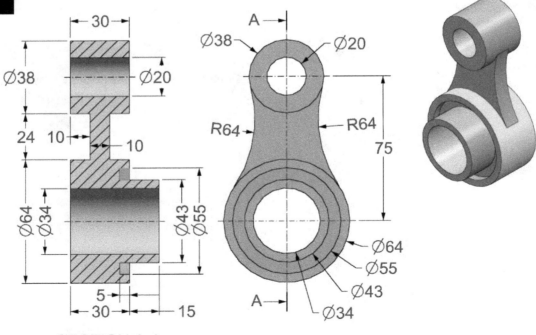

30
Ø38
Ø20
24 10
10
Ø64 Ø34
Ø43 Ø55
5
30
15

Ø38
Ø20
A
R64
R64
75
Ø64
Ø55
Ø43
Ø34
A

SECTION A-A
(SCALE 1:1)

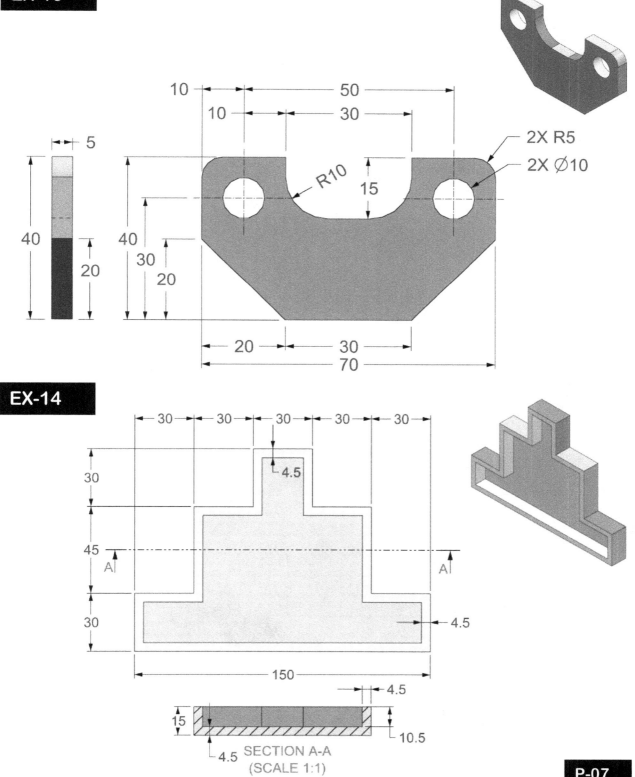

EX-13

10   50

10   30

2X R5

2X ⌀10

R10

15

5

40

40

30

20

20

20   30

70

EX-14

30   30   30   30   30

30

4.5

45

A   A

30

4.5

150

4.5

15

10.5

4.5   SECTION A-A
(SCALE 1:1)

P-07

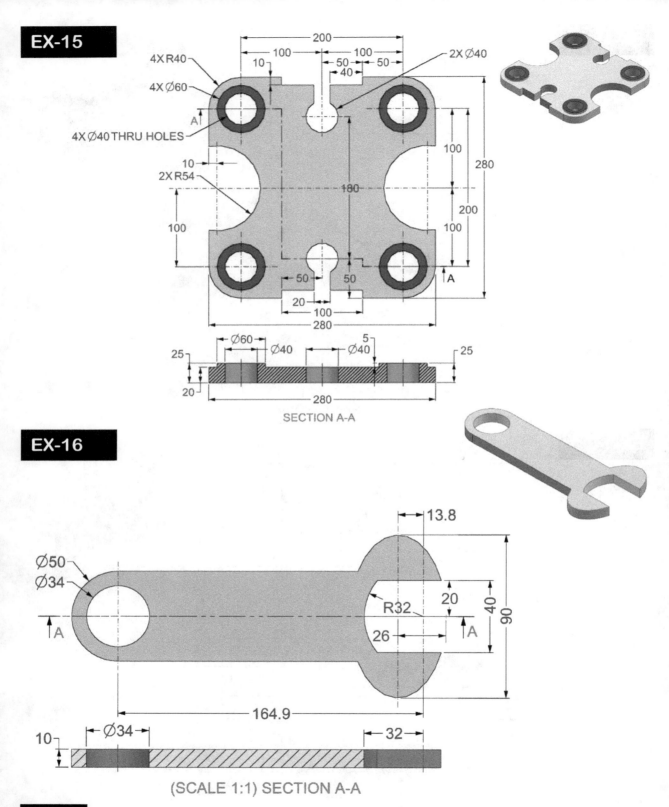

EX-15

4X R40
4X Ø60
4X Ø40 THRU HOLES
200
100
100
10
50
50
40
2X Ø40
A
10
2X R54
100
180
100
280
200
100
A
50
50
100
20
280

Ø60
Ø40
5
Ø40
25
25
20
280

SECTION A-A

EX-16

Ø50
Ø34
13.8
A
20
R32
40
90
26
A
164.9

10
Ø34
32

(SCALE 1:1) SECTION A-A

P-08

EX-17

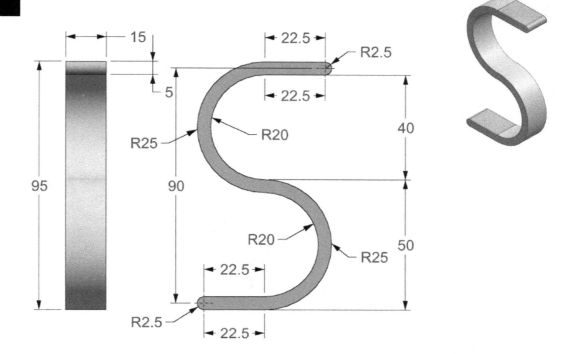

15

95

5

22.5

R2.5

22.5

R25

R20

40

90

R20

50

R25

22.5

R2.5

22.5

EX-18

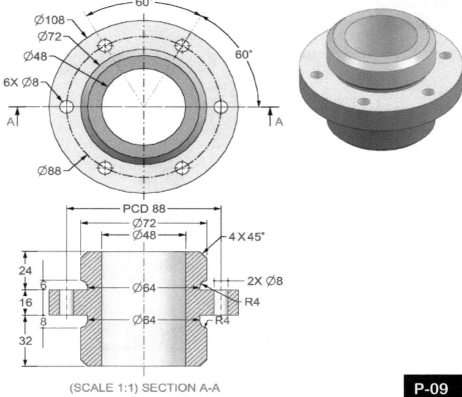

60°

Ø108

Ø72

Ø48

6X Ø8

60°

Ø88

A | | A

PCD 88

Ø72

Ø48

4 X 45°

24

6

Ø64

2X Ø8

16

R4

8

Ø64

R4

32

(SCALE 1:1) SECTION A-A

P-09

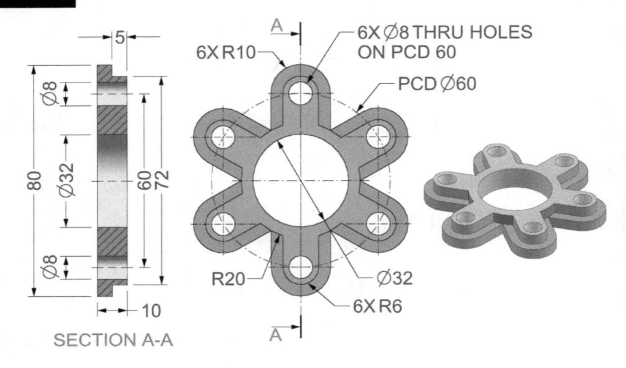

5

∅8

∅32

80

∅60

72

∅8

10

SECTION A-A

A

6X R10

6X ∅8 THRU HOLES
ON PCD 60

PCD ∅60

R20

∅32

6X R6

A

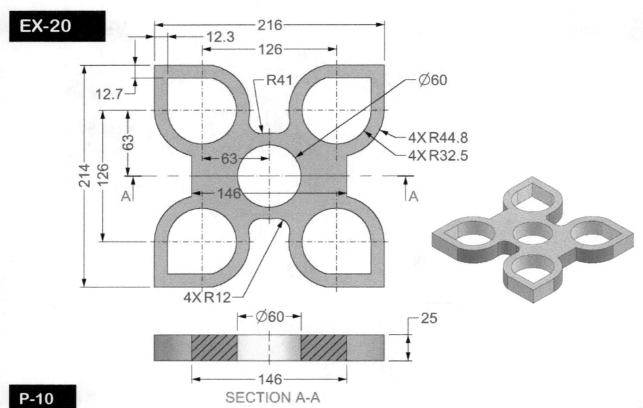

216

12.3

126

12.7

R41

∅60

63

63

4X R44.8
4X R32.5

214

126

A

146

A

4X R12

∅60

25

146

SECTION A-A

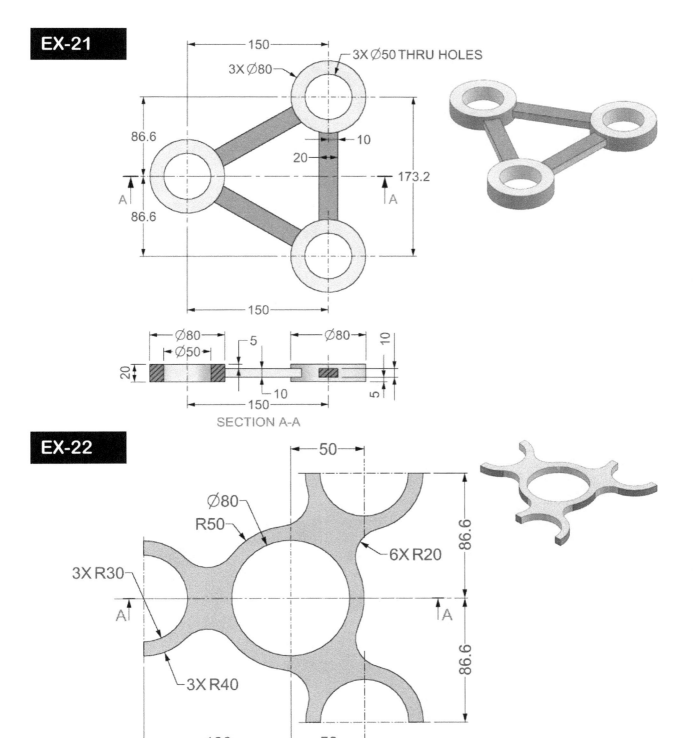

EX-21

150

3X Ø80
3X Ø50 THRU HOLES

86.6

10
20

173.2

A

A

86.6

150

Ø80
Ø50
5
Ø80
10
20
10
150
5

SECTION A-A

EX-22

50

Ø80
R50
6X R20

86.6

3X R30

A

A

86.6

3X R40

100
50

10
Ø80

SECTION A-A

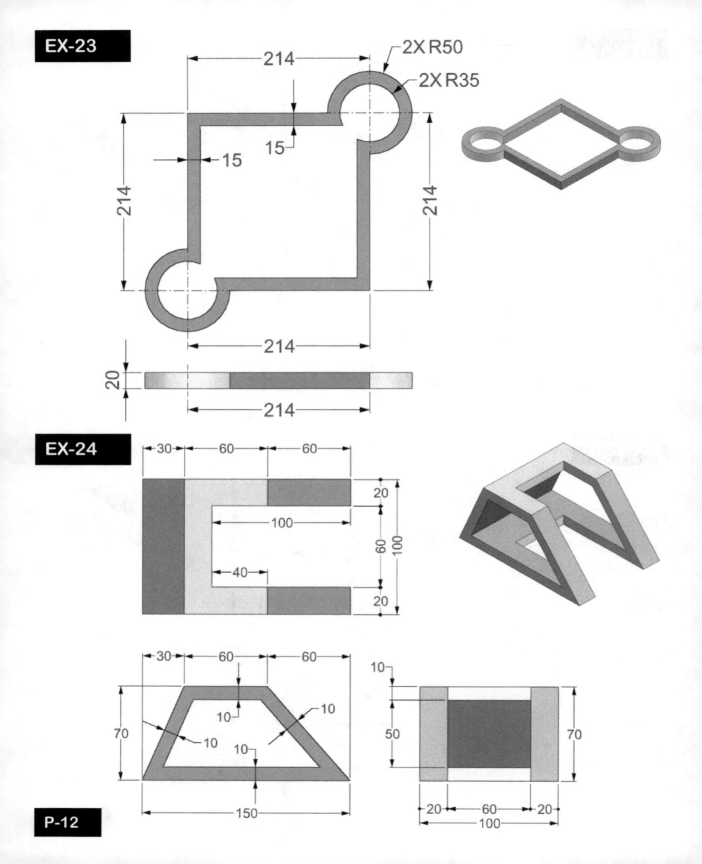

EX-23

214

2X R50

2X R35

15

15

214

214

214

20

214

EX-24

30 · 60 · 60

20

100

60 · 100

40

20

30 · 60 · 60

10

10

10

70

10

10

150

10

50

70

20 · 60 · 20

100

P-12

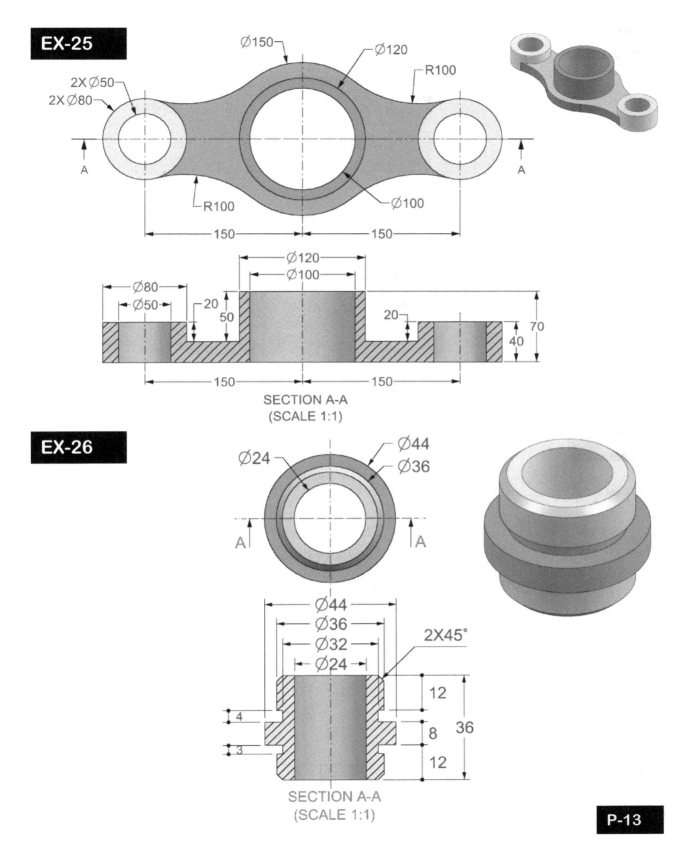

EX-25

Ø150 Ø120 R100

2X Ø50
2X Ø80

R100 Ø100

150 150

A A

Ø120
Ø100
Ø80
Ø50
20 50 20 70 40

150 150

SECTION A-A
(SCALE 1:1)

EX-26

Ø24 Ø44
Ø36

A A

Ø44
Ø36
Ø32
Ø24 2X45°

12
4 8 36
3 12

SECTION A-A
(SCALE 1:1)

EX-27

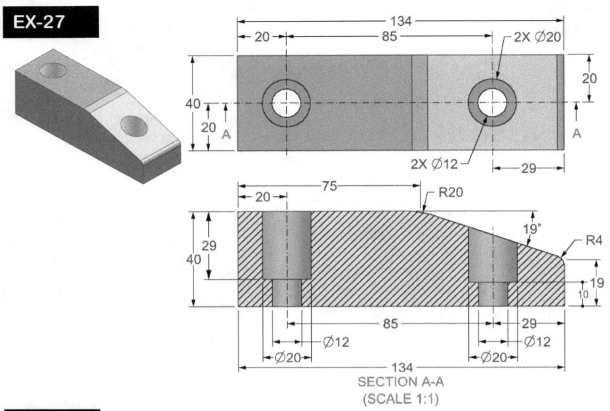

134
20
85
2X Ø20
40
20
20
A
A
20
2X Ø12
29

75
R20
20
19°
R4
29
40
19
10
85
29
Ø12
Ø12
Ø20
Ø20
134
SECTION A-A
(SCALE 1:1)

EX-28

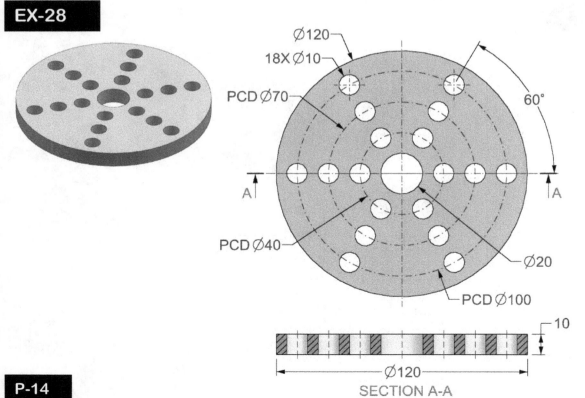

Ø120
18X Ø10
PCD Ø70
60°
A
A
PCD Ø40
Ø20
PCD Ø100
10
Ø120
SECTION A-A

EX-29

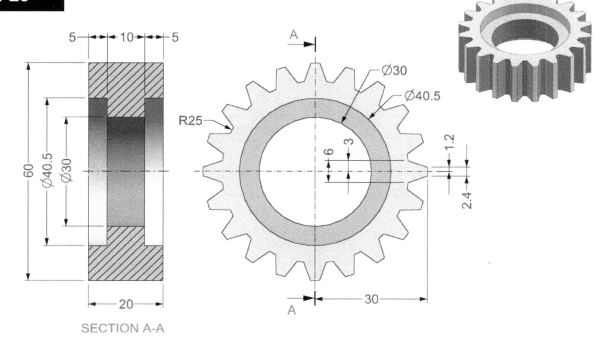

SECTION A-A

EX-30

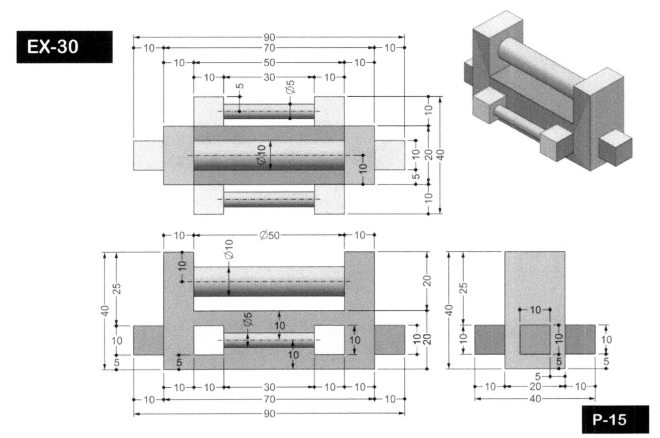

P-15

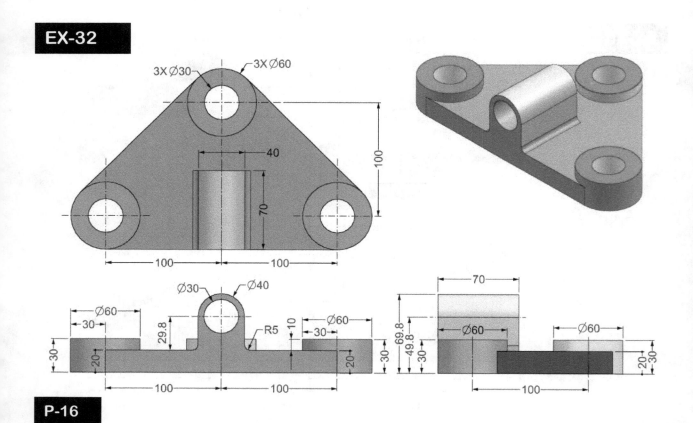

EX-31

40
Ø20

Ø20
Ø16

40

R5
R2

R2

15
10

60
100

SECTION A-A

60
20 40

Ø40

Ø40
Ø20

Ø20

A

A

Ø16

60
20

40

Ø20

R5

R2

15
10

60 20

40

40
30

R2

15
10

20

EX-32

3X Ø30

3X Ø60

40

100

70

100 100

Ø30 Ø40

Ø60
30

29.8

R5

10

Ø60
30

20

20

30

100 100

70

69.8
49.8
30

Ø60

Ø60

20
30

100

P-16

EX-33

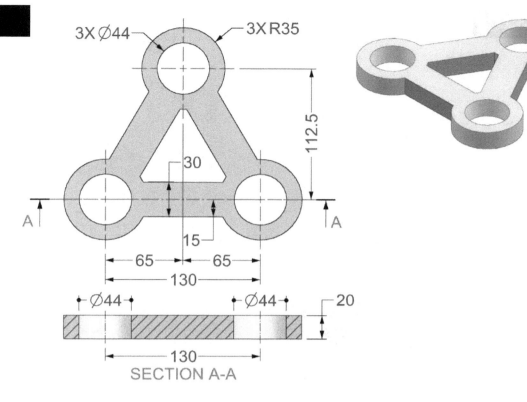

3X Ø44   3X R35

112.5

30

15

65   65

130

Ø44   Ø44   20

130

SECTION A-A

EX-34

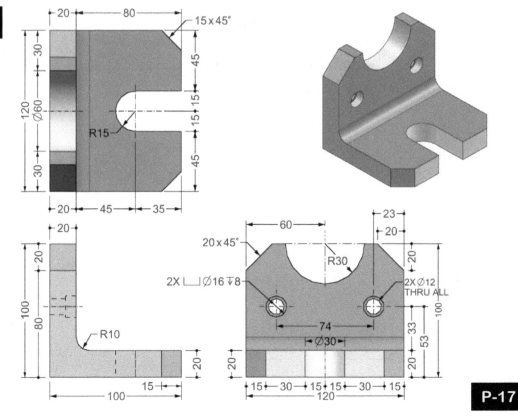

20   80   15 x 45°

30

120   Ø60   45

R15   15 15

15 15

30   45

20   45   35

20

20

100   80

R10

20

15

100

20 x 45°   60   23

20

R30

2X ⌴ Ø16 ↧8   20

2X Ø12
THRU ALL

74

100

Ø30   33

53

20

20   15 30 15 15 30 15

120

P-17

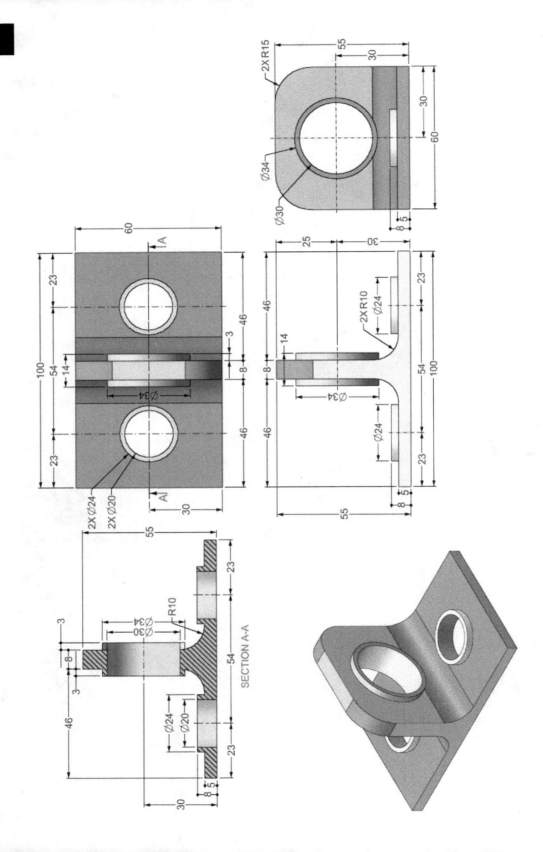

SECTION A-A

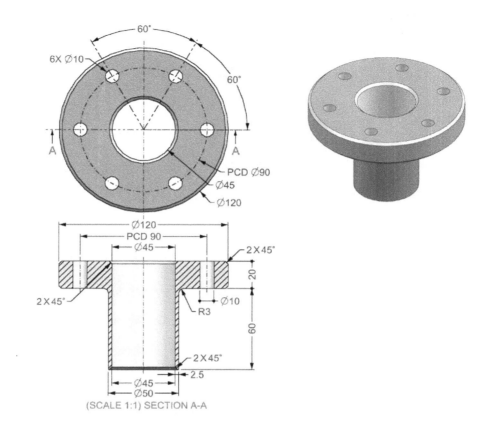

6X Ø10
60°
60°
PCD Ø90
Ø45
Ø120

Ø120
PCD 90
Ø45
2 X 45°
20
2 X 45°
Ø10
R3
60
2 X 45°
2.5
Ø45
Ø50
(SCALE 1:1) SECTION A-A

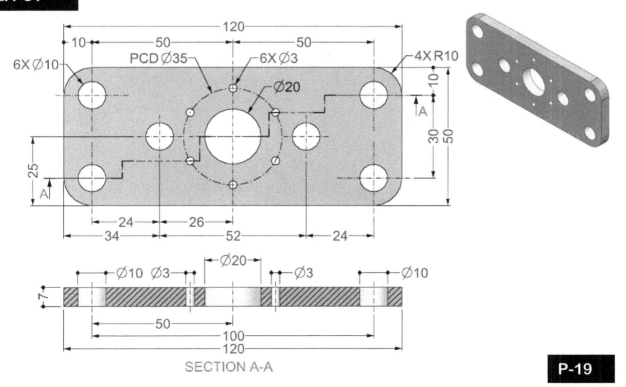

120
10
50
50
6X Ø10
PCD Ø35
6X Ø3
4X R10
Ø20
10
A
30
50
25
A
24
26
34
52
24

Ø10   Ø3
Ø20
Ø3
Ø10
7
50
100
120
SECTION A-A

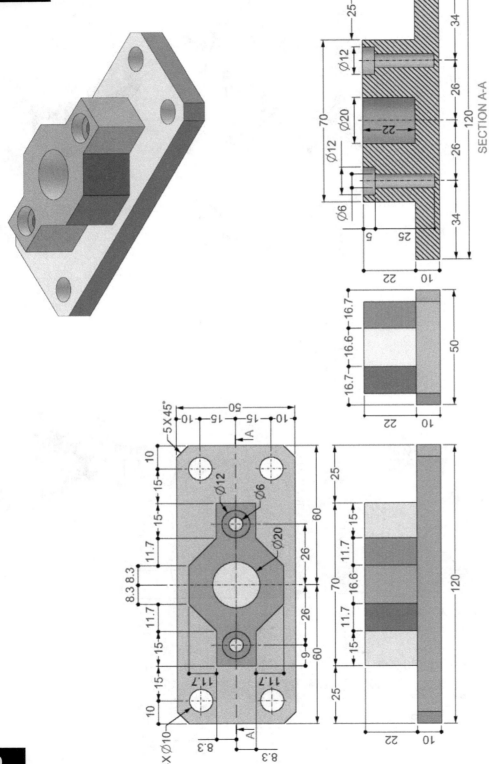

SECTION A-A

EX-39

70

R20
Ø20

40

45

R25
Ø20

45

20

30

A —— A

10

10

45

65

20

2X R10
Ø40
Ø20

25

45

SECTION A-A

EX-40

Ø60

20

10

5

Ø50

Ø60
Ø50

5 —10— 5

30

Ø60

20

P-21

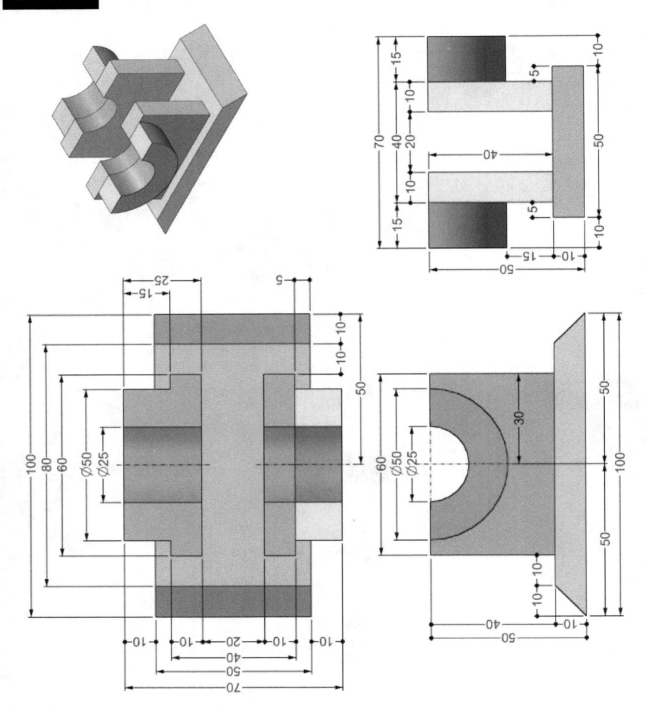

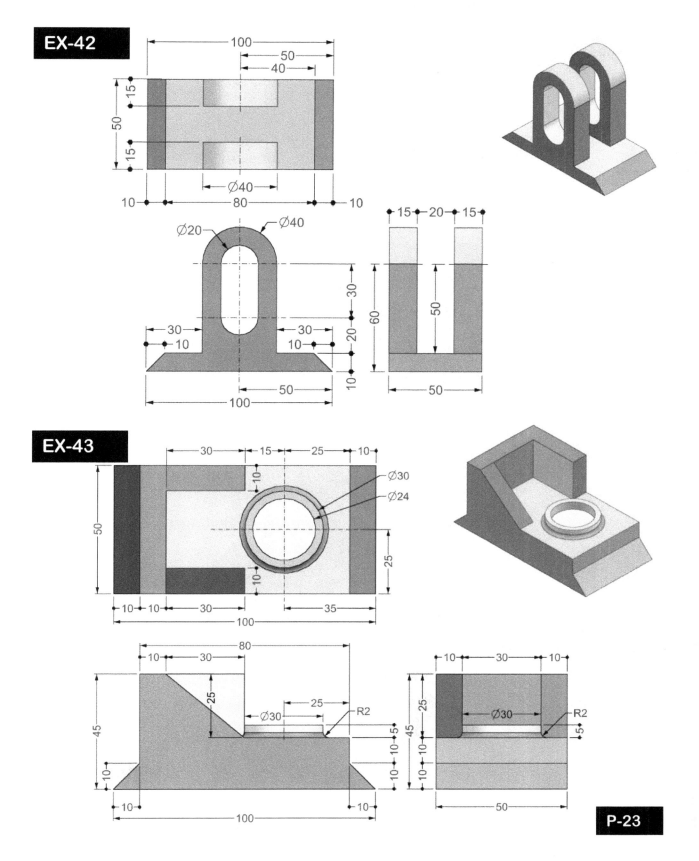

EX-42

EX-43

P-23

EX-44

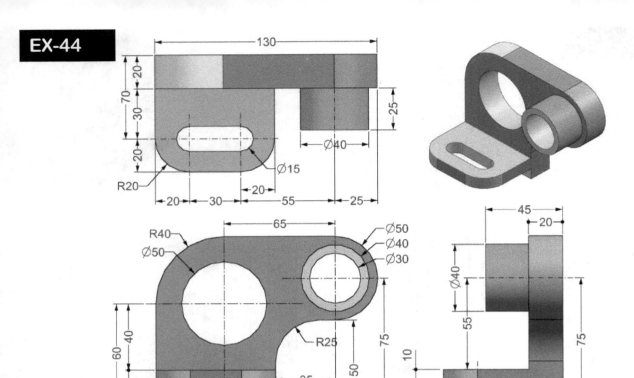

EX-45

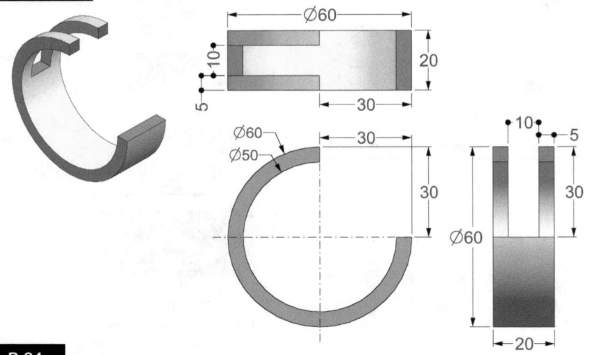

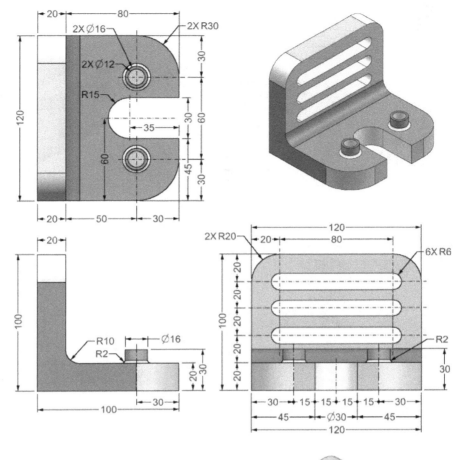

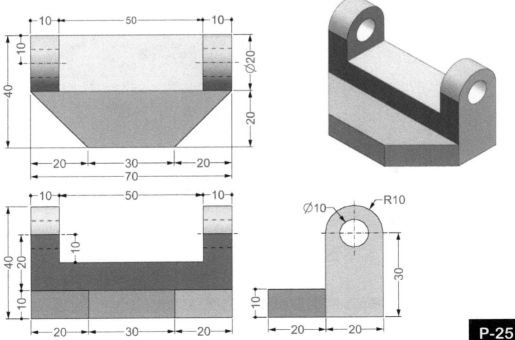

EX-48

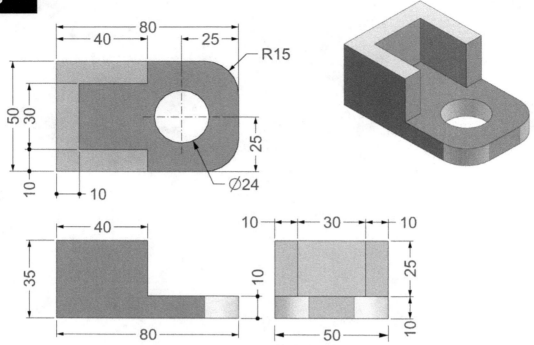

EX-49

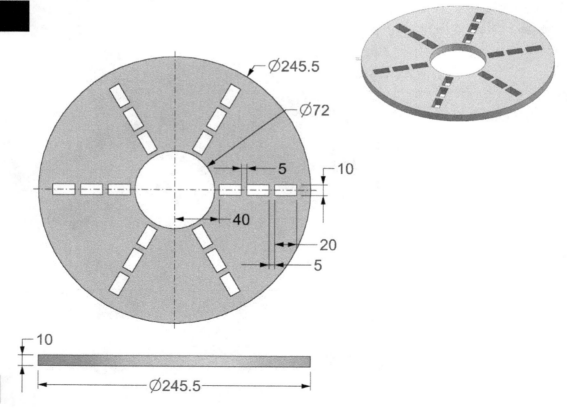

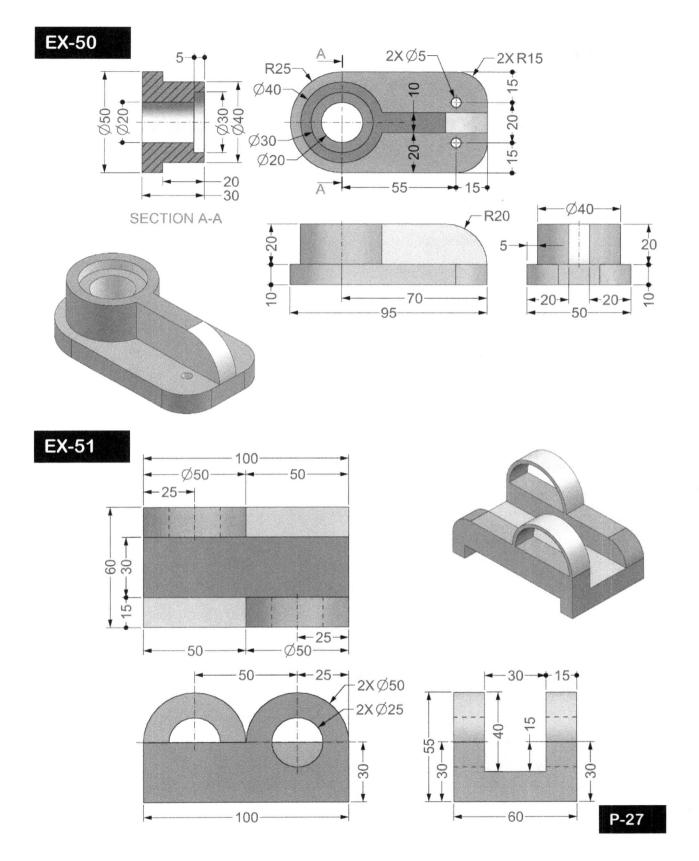

EX-50

R25
Ø40
Ø30
Ø20
5
Ø50
Ø20
Ø30
Ø40
20
30
SECTION A-A

A
2X Ø5
2X R15
10
15
20
15
20
55
15

R20
20
10
70
95

Ø40
5
20
20
20
50
10

EX-51

100
Ø50
50
25
60
30
15
50
Ø50
25

2X Ø50
2X Ø25

50
25
30
100

30
15
55
40
30
15
30
60

P-27

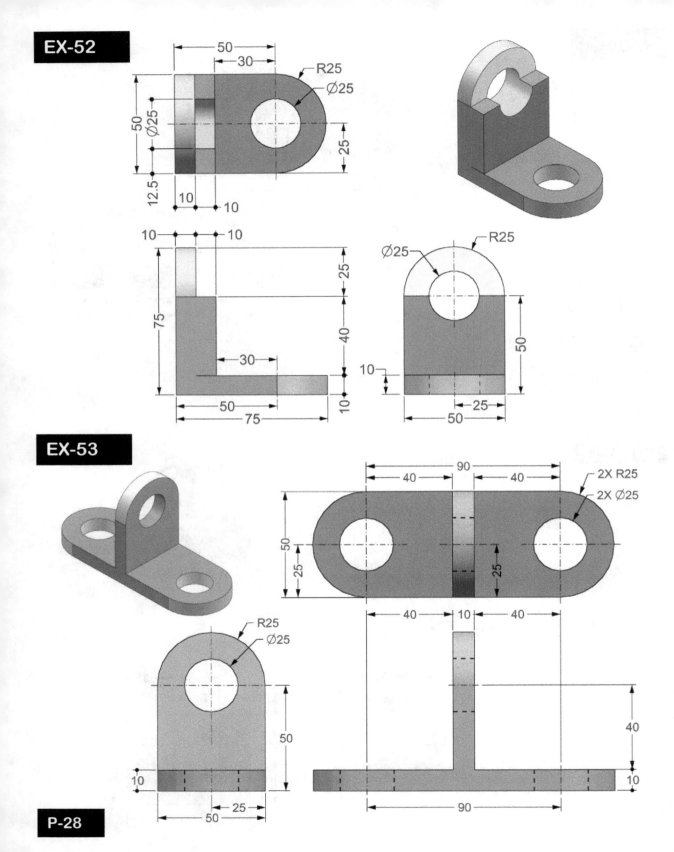

EX-52

EX-53

EX-54

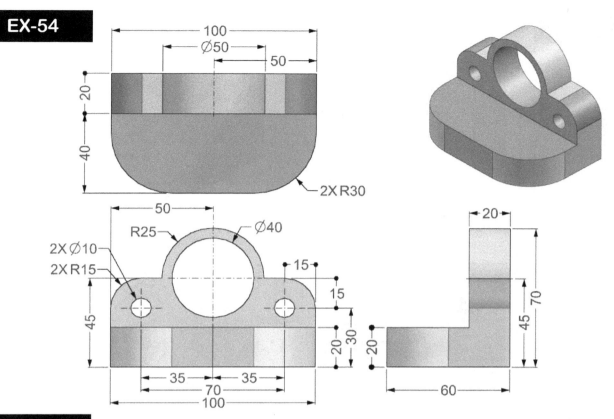

EX-55

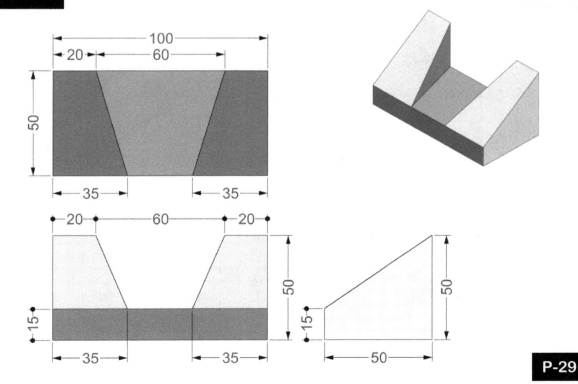

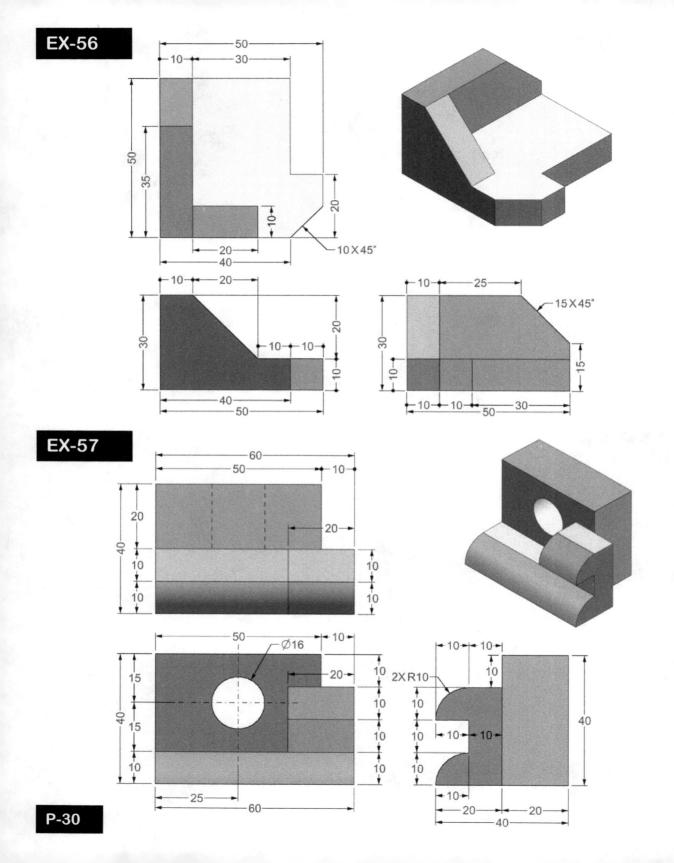

EX-56

50
10 30
50
35
20
20
10
40
10 X 45°

10 20
30
20
10 10
10
40
50

10 25
15 X 45°
30
10
15
10 10 30
50

EX-57

60
50 10
20
40
20
10 10
10 10
10 10

50 Ø16
10
15
20 10
40
10
15
10
10 10
25
60

10 10
10
2X R10
10
10 10
40
10
10 10
20 20
40

P-30

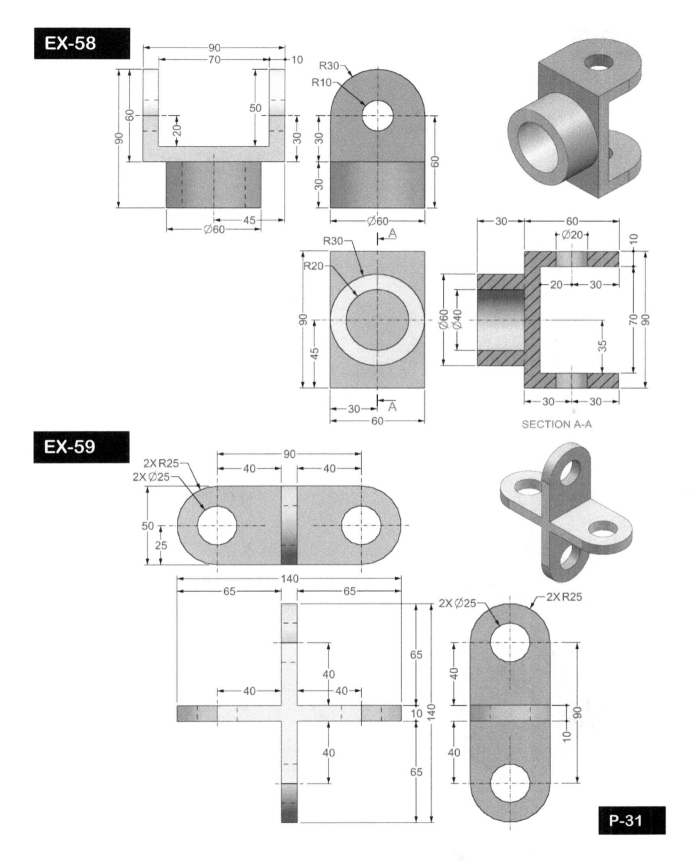

EX-58

R30
R10

90
70
10
60
90
50
20
30
30
45
Ø60

R30
R20
90
45
30
60

A
Ø60
30
30
60

30
60
Ø20
10
Ø60
Ø40
20
30
70
90
35
30
30

SECTION A-A

EX-59

2X R25
2X Ø25
90
40
40
50
25

140
65
65
65
40
40
40
10
40
65

2X Ø25
2X R25
40
90
10
40

P-31

EX-60

Top view dimensions: Ø50, 22.5, 2X Ø10, 15, 25, 60, 43.9, 10, 25, 15, 50, 45, 95

Front view dimensions: Ø50, Ø40, R4, R10, R10, 10, R10, 40, 10, 45, 45, R10, R10, 155, 130, 80, 140, 30, 55, 40, 10, 22.5, 55, 10, 22.5, 100

Side view dimensions: 60, 85.4, 100, 155, 34.6, 10, 25, 40, 60

EX-61

Front view dimensions: Ø120, 20, R3, Ø50, 50, R2, 10, 10, 10, Ø50, Ø70

Top/bottom view dimensions: 14, 14, PCD Ø90, Ø70, Ø50, R60, Ø30, 6X Ø10, 66, 132, 14, 14, A, A, 66, 66, 132

SECTION A-A dimensions: 132, Ø70, Ø50, Ø30, 10, 10, Ø10, 10, 10, R2, Ø50, Ø30, 50, 100, Ø10, R3, 45, 45, 20, 90, Ø120

Right view dimensions: Ø120, PCD Ø90, 6X Ø10 ON PCD 90, Ø30, 66, 132, 14, 14, 14, 14, 66, 14, 14, 66, 132

SECTION A-A

P-32

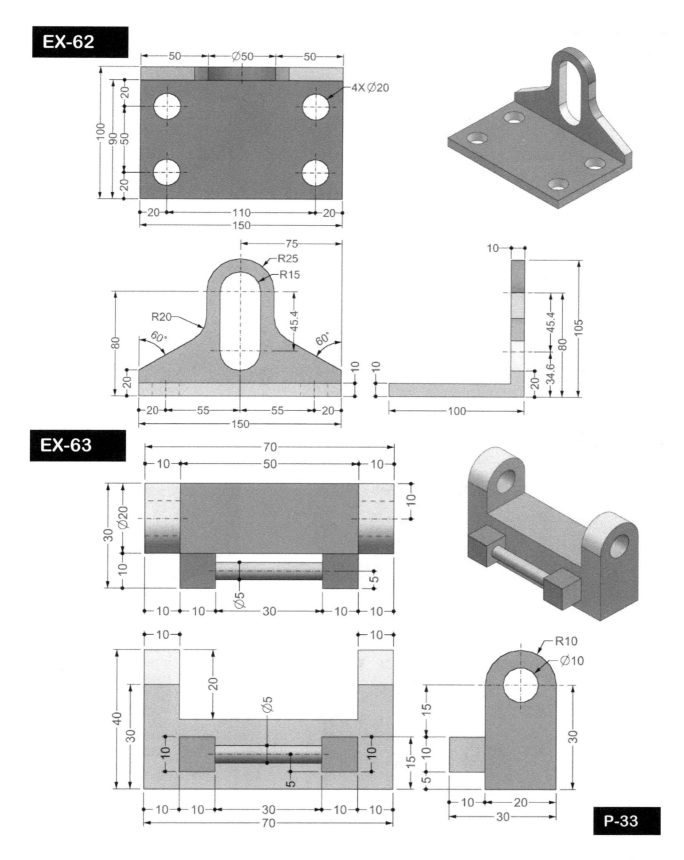

EX-62

EX-63

P-33

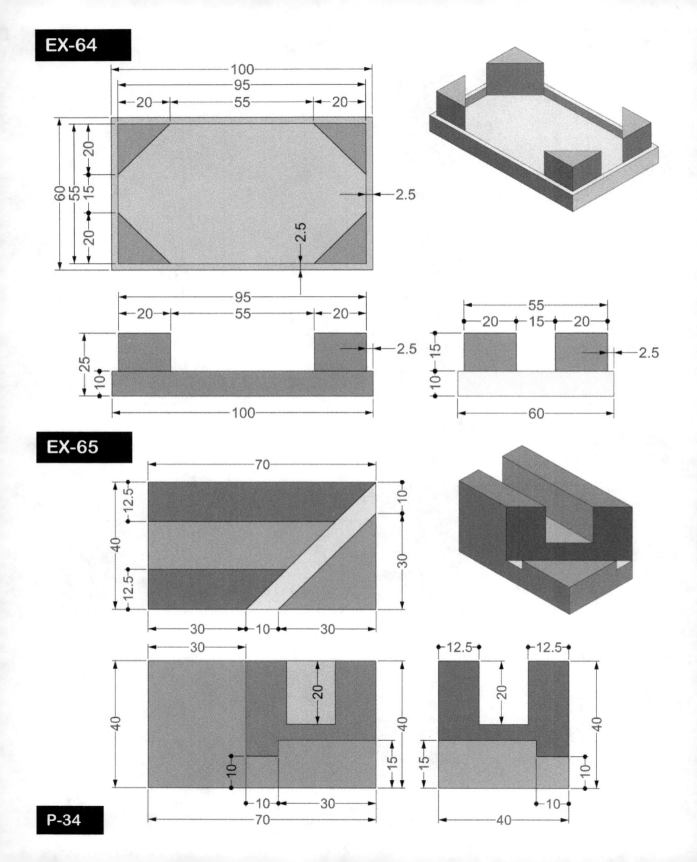

EX-64

EX-65

P-34

EX-66

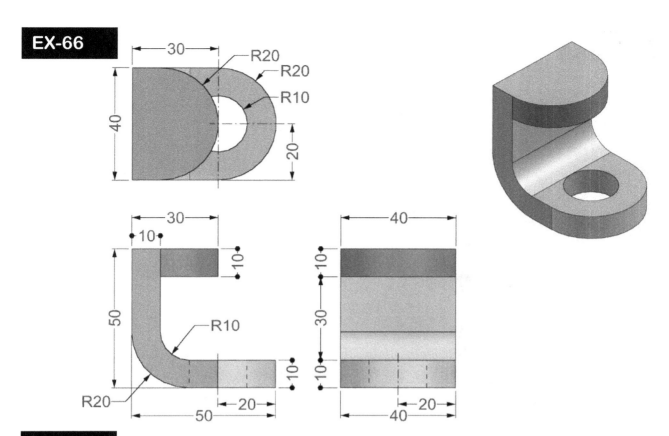

EX-67

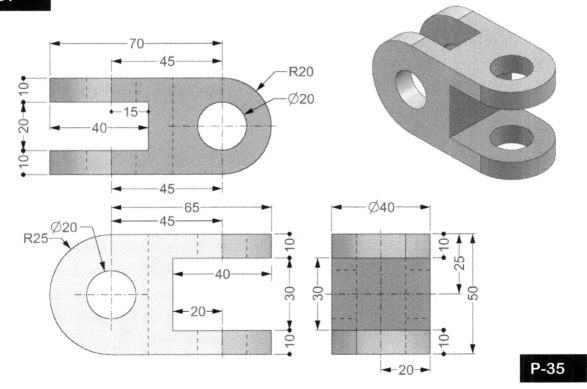

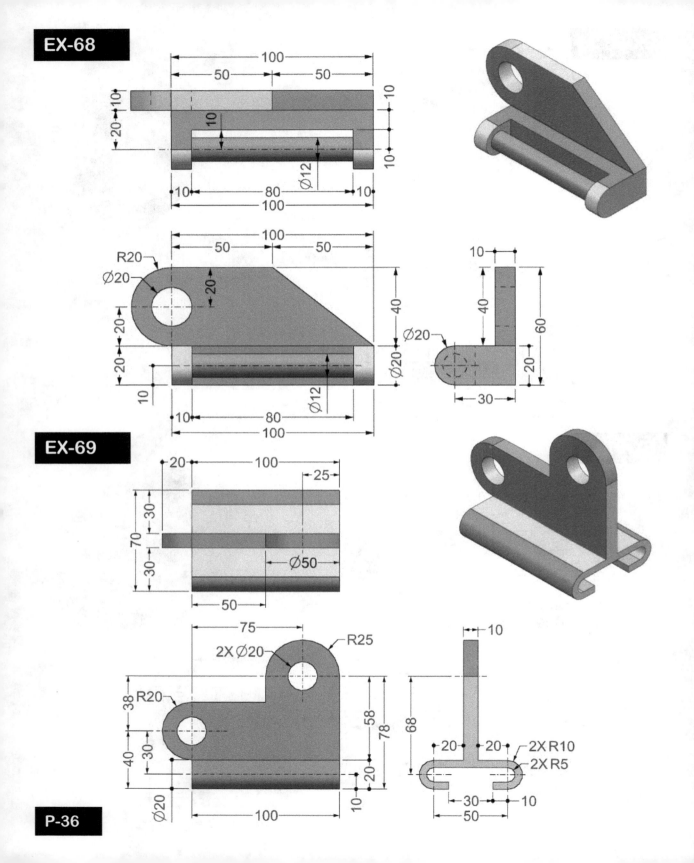

EX-68

EX-69

P-36

EX-70

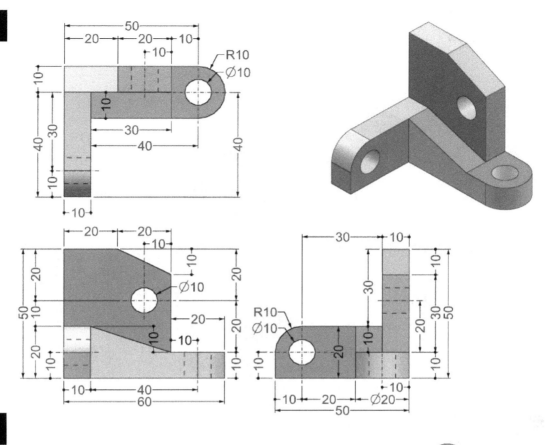

EX-71

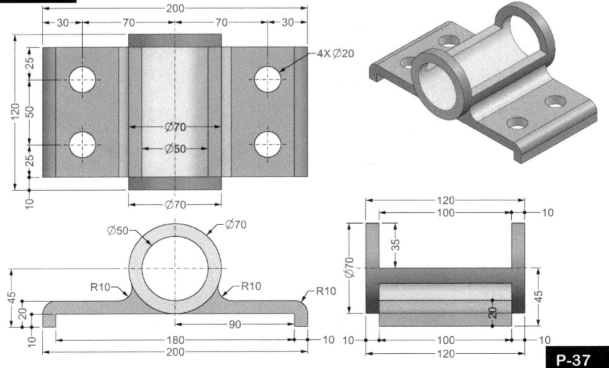

P-37

EX-72

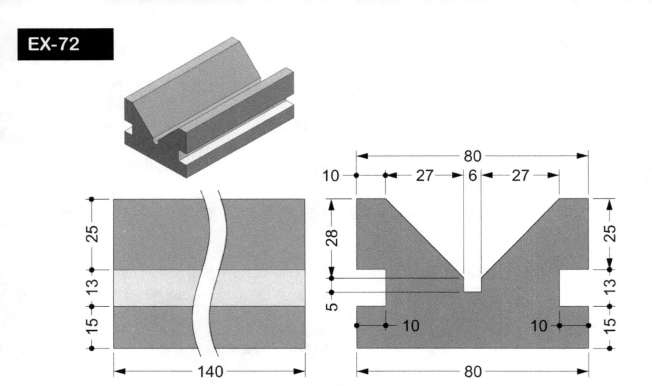

EX-73

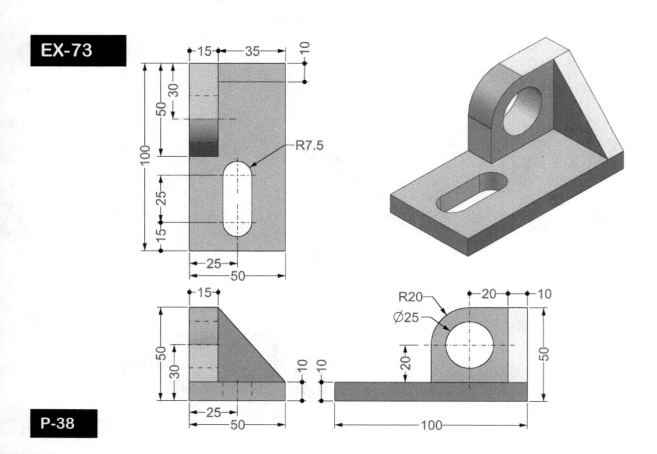

R7.5

R20

Ø25

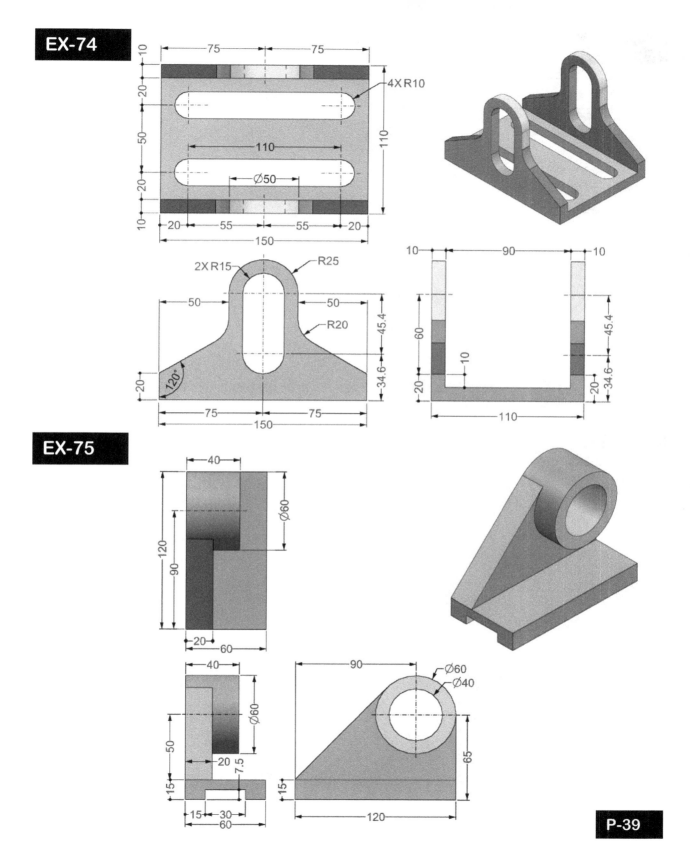

EX-74

75 75
10
20
50
20
10
4X R10
110
110
Ø50
20 55 55 20
150

2X R15 R25
50 50
45.4
R20
120°
20
34.6
75 75
150

10 90 10
60
10
45.4
20 34.6
20
110

EX-75

40
120
90
Ø60
20
60

40
Ø60
50
20 7.5
15
15 30
60

90 Ø60
Ø40
65
15
120

EX-76

R20
Ø28
120
70
10
40
20
40
10
50

70
10
15
R25
Ø30
15
10
50
70

25
20
Ø40

EX-77

R15
R25
50
R10
A — A
R5

SECTION A-A
Ø30
50
R1
30
20
30
R4
R2
Ø10
5

P-40

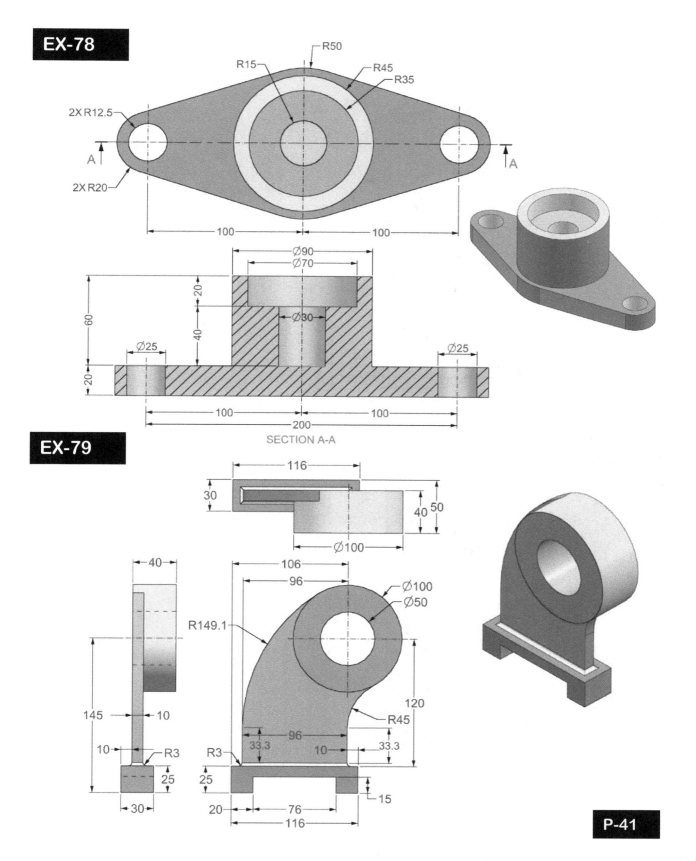

EX-78

R50
R15
R45
R35
2X R12.5
2X R20
A
A
100
100

Ø90
Ø70
20
60
40
Ø30
Ø25
Ø25
20
100
100
200
SECTION A-A

EX-79

116
30
40 50
Ø100

40
106
96
Ø100
Ø50
R149.1
120
R45
145
10
10
R3
R3
96
33.3
10
33.3
25
25
30
20
76
15
116

P-41

EX-80

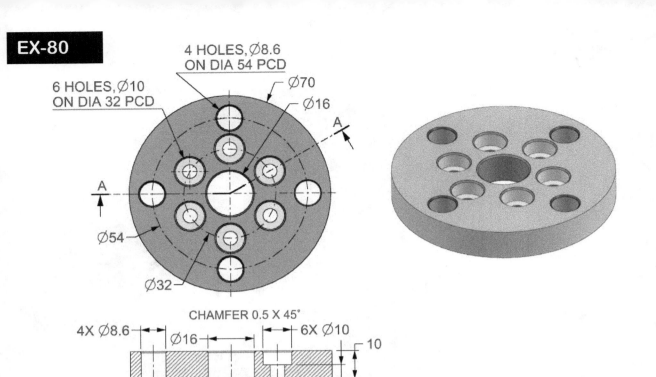

6 HOLES,Ø10
ON DIA 32 PCD

4 HOLES,Ø8.6
ON DIA 54 PCD

Ø70

Ø16

A

A

Ø54

Ø32

CHAMFER 0.5 X 45°

4X Ø8.6

Ø16

6X Ø10

10

5

5

SECTION A-A
(SCALE 1:1)

EX-81

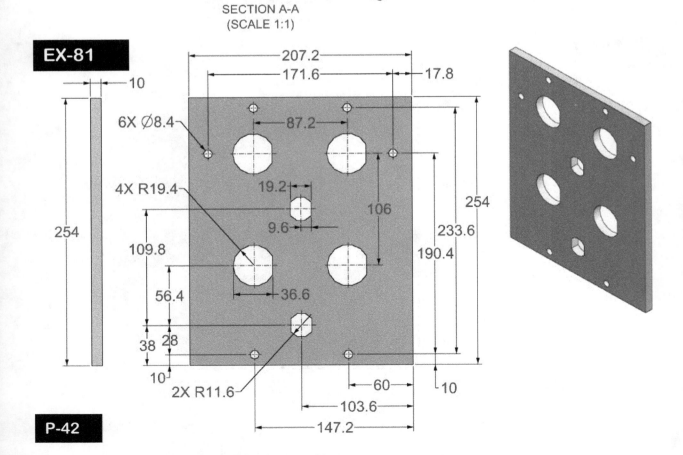

10

207.2

171.6

17.8

6X Ø8.4

87.2

4X R19.4

19.2

106

254

9.6

233.6

254

109.8

190.4

56.4

36.6

38 28

2X R11.6

60

10

103.6

10

147.2

P-42

EX-82

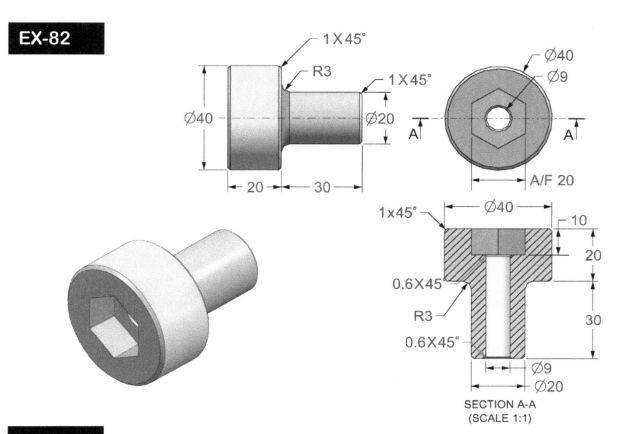

1 X 45°
R3
1 X 45°
Ø40
Ø20
20
30

Ø40
Ø9
A
A
A/F 20

1x45°
Ø40
10
20
0.6X45°
R3
30
0.6X45°
Ø9
Ø20

SECTION A-A
(SCALE 1:1)

EX-83

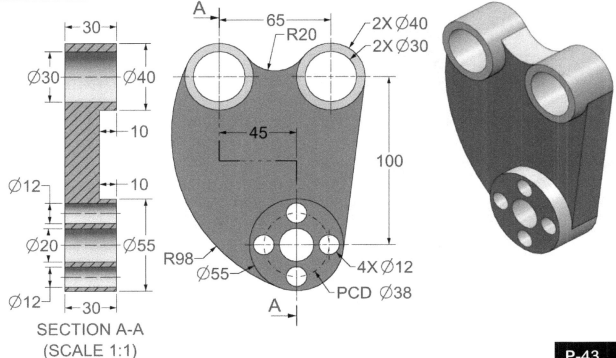

30
Ø30
Ø40
10
10
Ø12
Ø20
Ø55
R98
Ø55
Ø12
30

SECTION A-A
(SCALE 1:1)

A
65
R20
2X Ø40
2X Ø30
45
100
4X Ø12
PCD Ø38
A

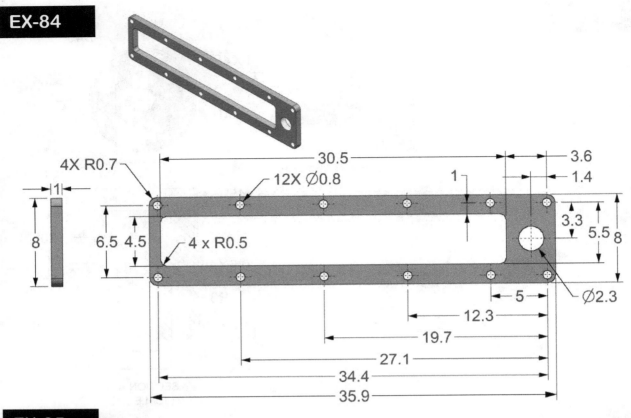

4X R0.7
12X Ø0.8
4 x R0.5
30.5
3.6
1.4
1
3.3
5.5
8
1
8
6.5 4.5
Ø2.3
5
12.3
19.7
27.1
34.4
35.9

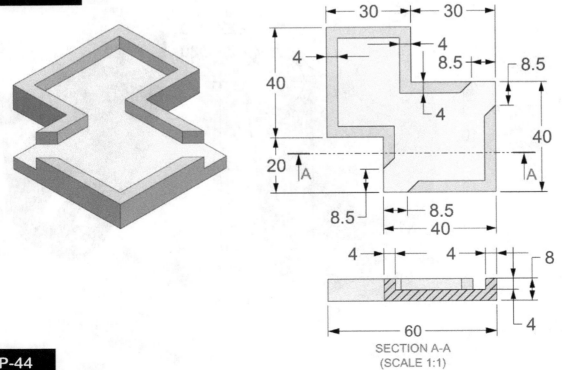

30
30
4
4
8.5
8.5
40
4
40
20
A
8.5
8.5
40
A
4
4
8
60
SECTION A-A
(SCALE 1:1)

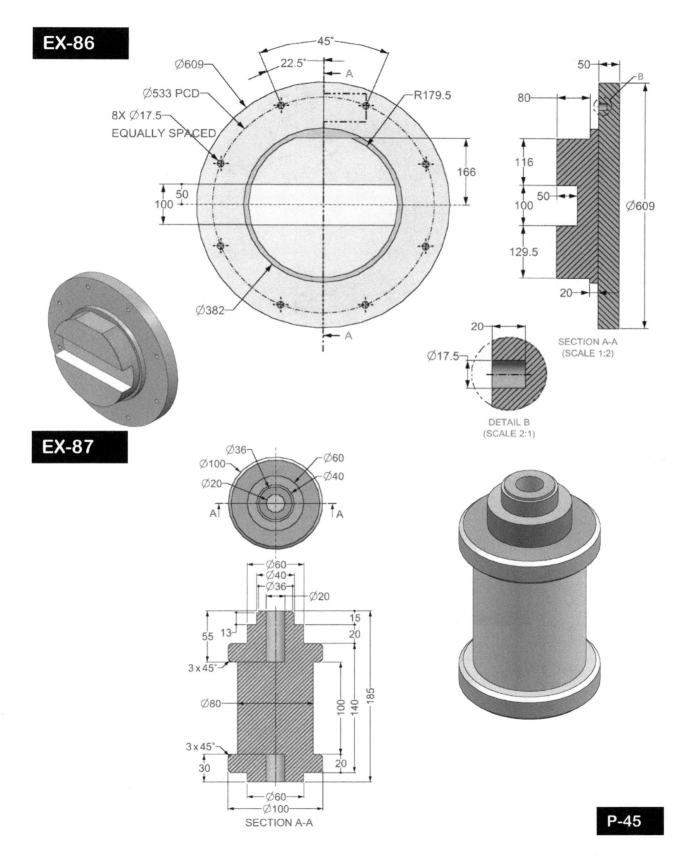

EX-86

∅609
∅533 PCD
8X ∅17.5
EQUALLY SPACED
45°
22.5°
A
R179.5
166
50
100
∅382

50
80
B
116
100
50
∅609
129.5
20

SECTION A-A
(SCALE 1:2)

20
∅17.5

DETAIL B
(SCALE 2:1)

EX-87

∅36
∅60
∅100
∅40
∅20
A   A

∅60
∅40
∅36
∅20
13
15
55
20
3 x 45°
∅80
100
140
185
3 x 45°
30
20
∅60
∅100

SECTION A-A

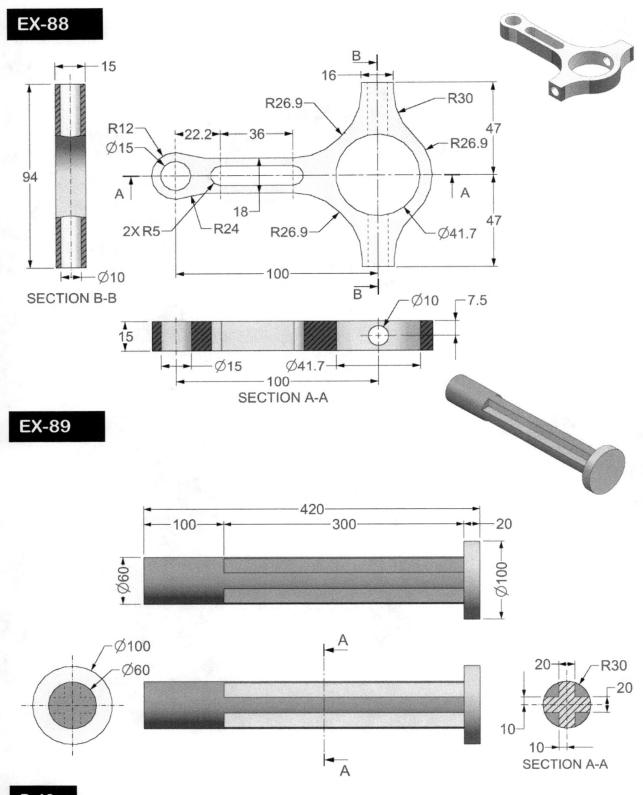

EX-88

SECTION B-B

15

94

Ø10

R12
Ø15

22.2   36

2X R5   R24

18

B

16   R30

R26.9

R26.9

47

47

R26.9   Ø41.7

100

B

A   A

Ø10   7.5

15

Ø15   Ø41.7

100

SECTION A-A

EX-89

420

100   300   20

Ø60   Ø100

Ø100
Ø60

A

A

20   R30

20

10

10

SECTION A-A

P-46

EX-90

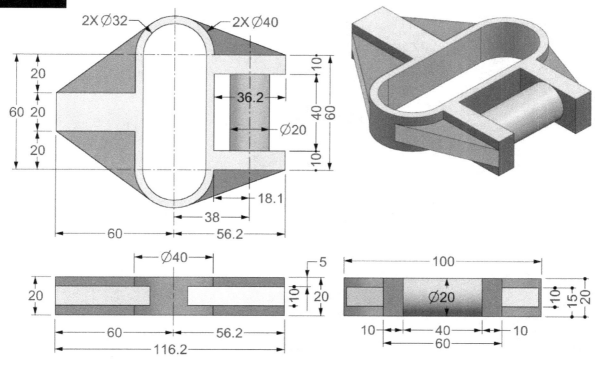

EX-91

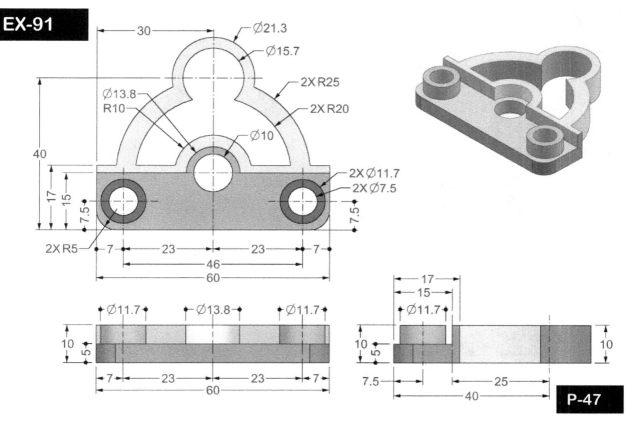

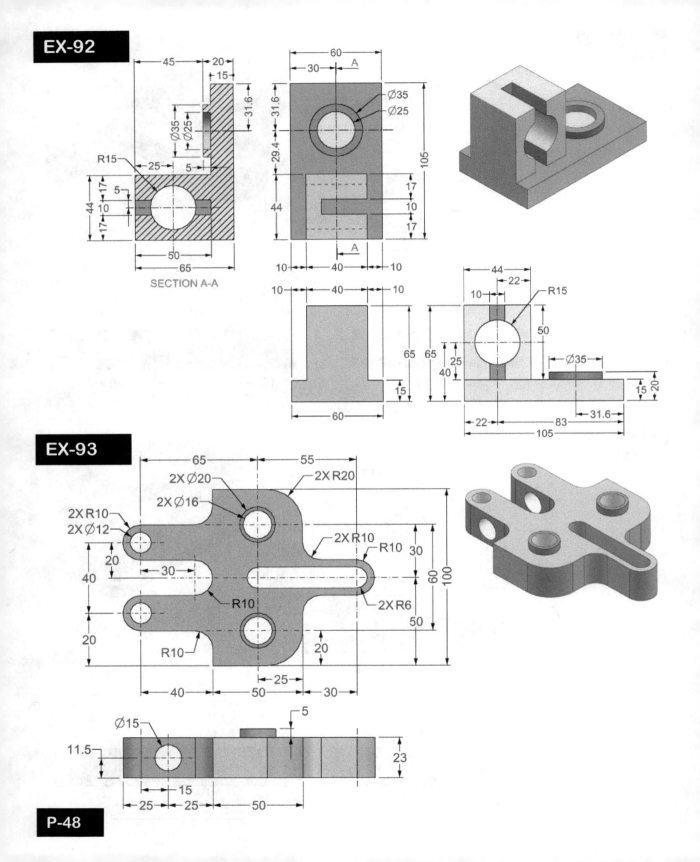

EX-92

SECTION A-A

EX-93

P-48

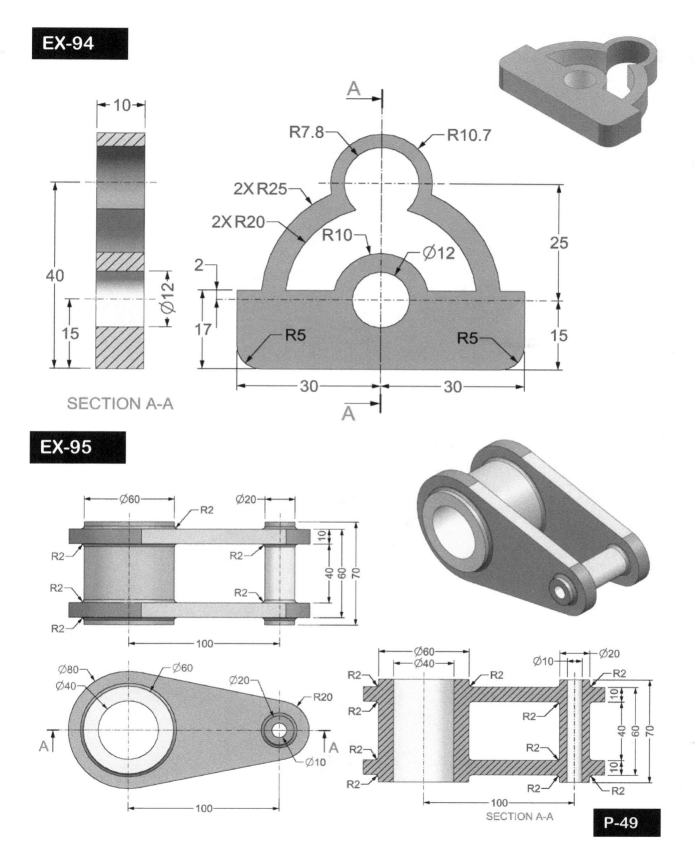

EX-94

R7.8   R10.7

2X R25

2X R20   R10   Ø12

10

40   Ø12

15

2

17

R5   R5

30   30

25

15

SECTION A-A

A
A

EX-95

Ø60   Ø20   R2

R2   R2

10
40
60
70

R2   R2

100

Ø80   Ø60   Ø20   R20

Ø40

A   A

Ø10

100

Ø60   Ø10   Ø20

Ø40

R2   R2

R2   R2

10
40
60
70

R2   R2

R2   R2

100
SECTION A-A

P-49

EX-96

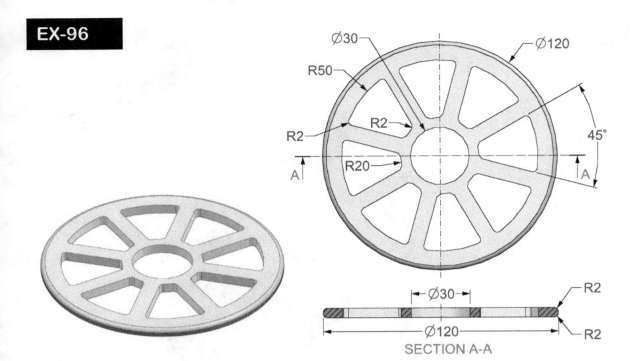

Ø30
Ø120
R50
R2
R2
R20
45°
A
A

Ø30
R2
Ø120
R2
SECTION A-A

EX-97

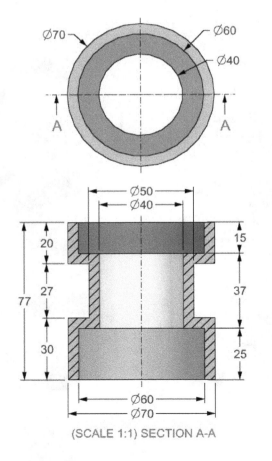

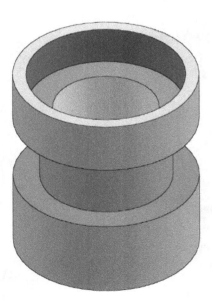

Ø70
Ø60
Ø40
A
A

Ø50
Ø40
20
15
27
37
77
30
25
Ø60
Ø70
(SCALE 1:1) SECTION A-A

P-50

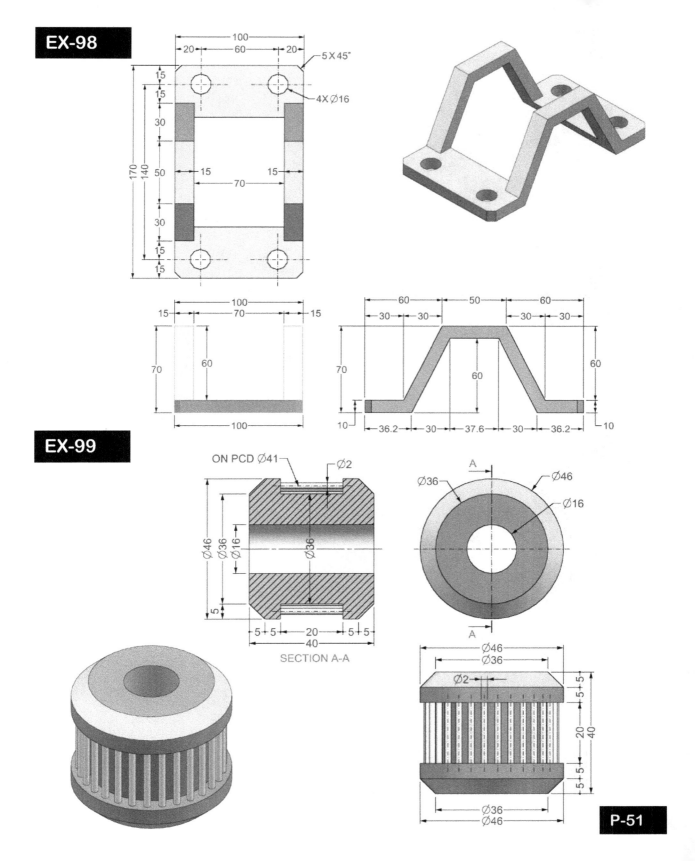

EX-98

EX-99

ON PCD Ø41

SECTION A-A

P-51

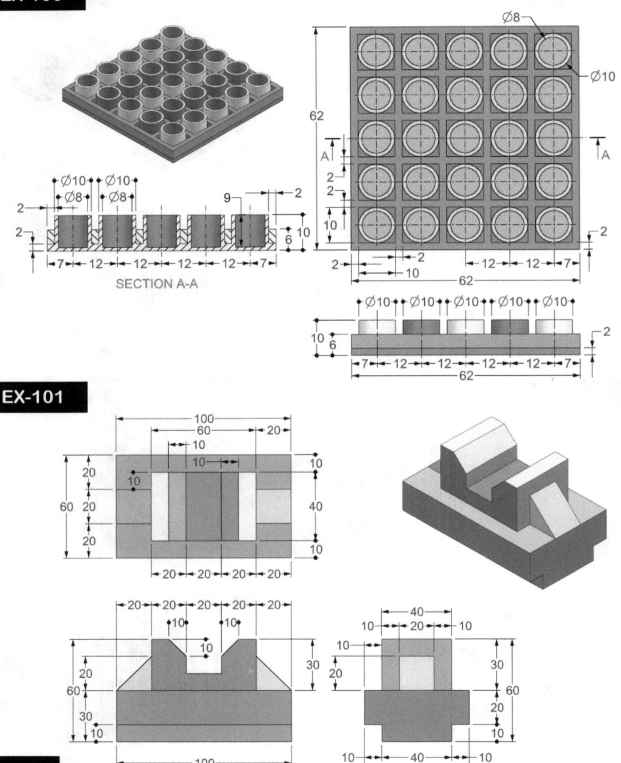

EX-100

SECTION A-A

EX-101

P-52

EX-102

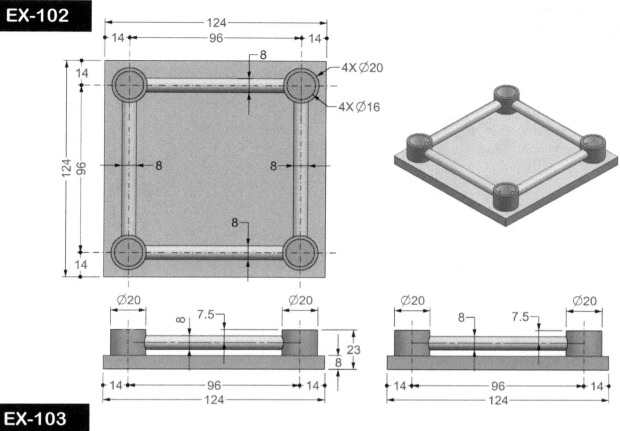

EX-103

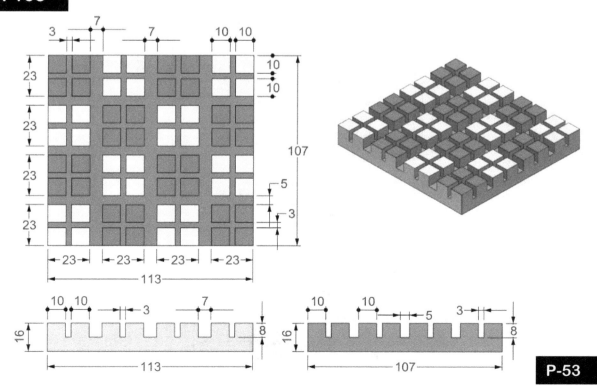

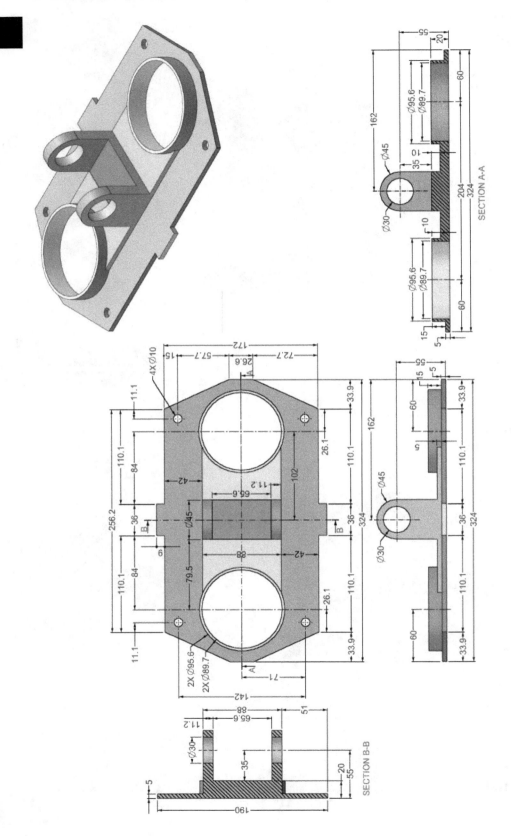

SECTION A-A

SECTION B-B

EX-105

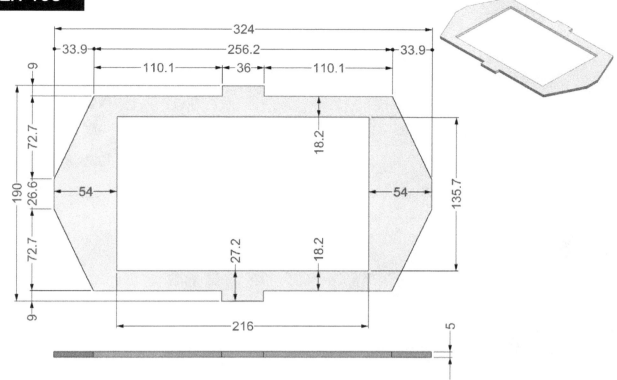

EX-106

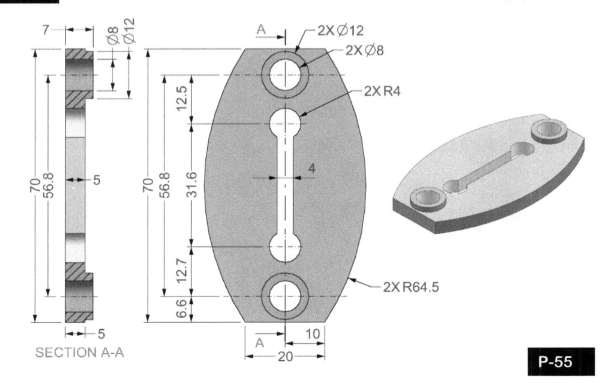

SECTION A-A

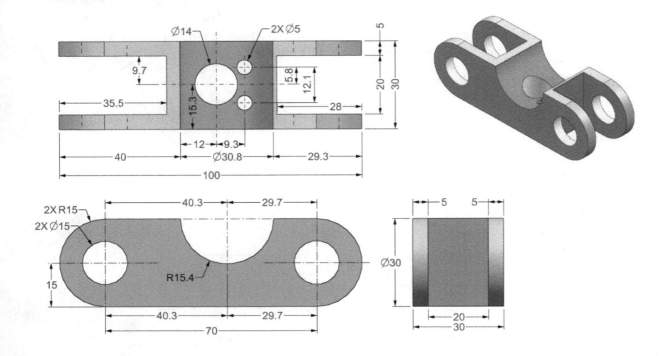

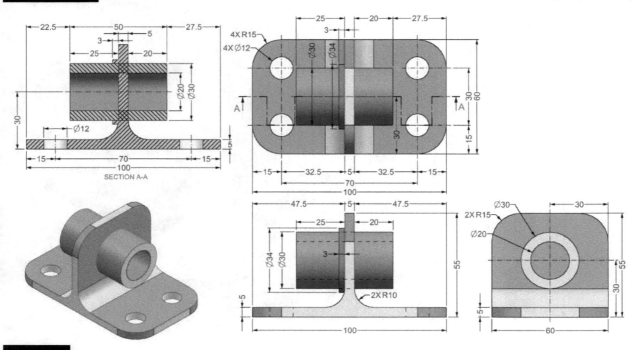

SECTION A-A

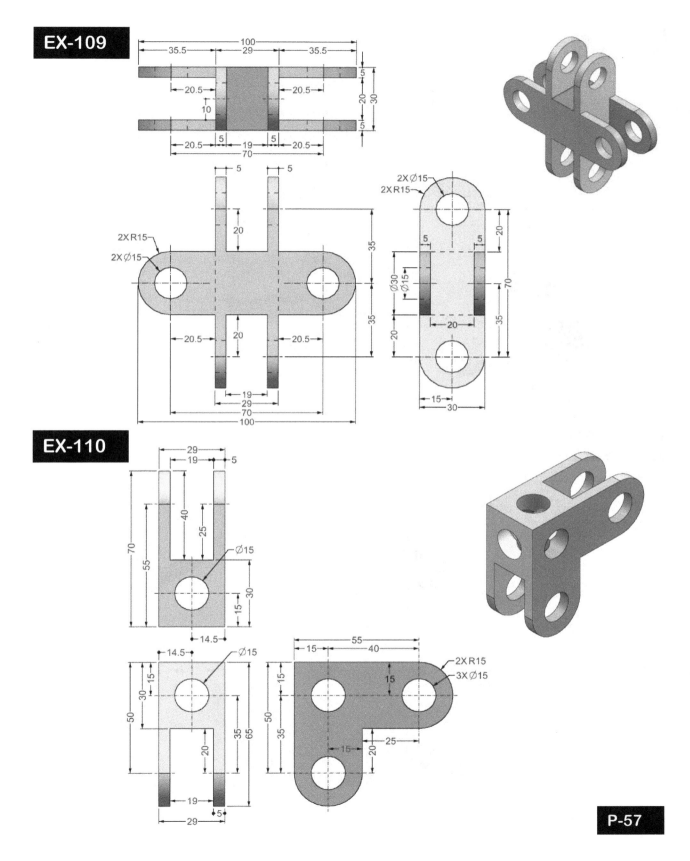

EX-109

EX-110

P-57

EX-111

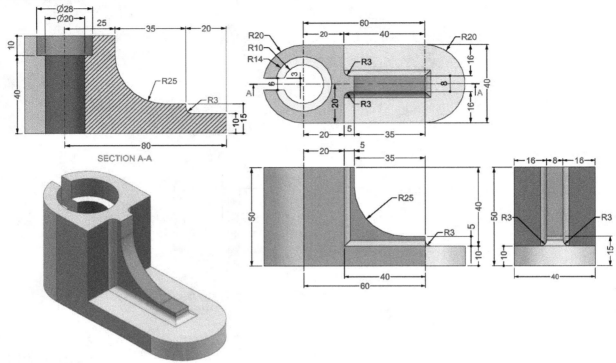

SECTION A-A

EX-112

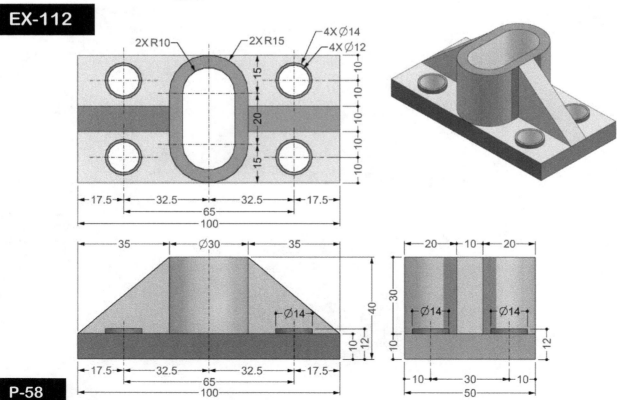

EX-113

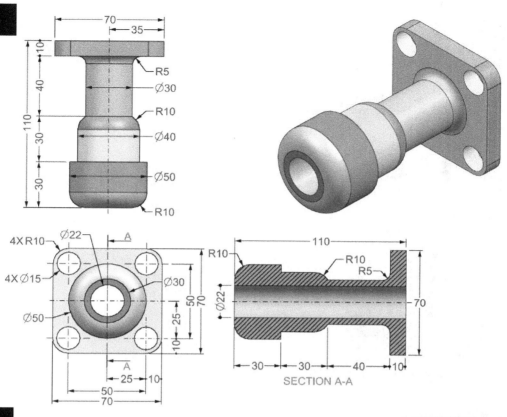

4X R10
Ø22
A
4X Ø15
Ø30
Ø50
50
70
25
10
A
25 10
50
70

R10
110
R10
R5
Ø22
70
30 30 40 10
SECTION A-A

EX-114

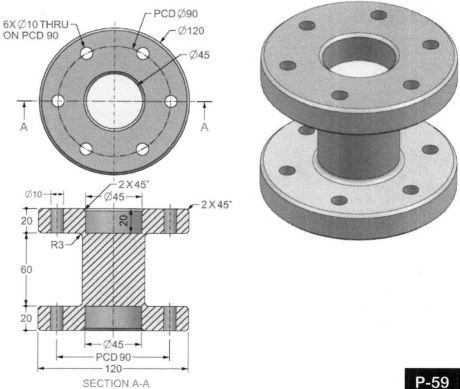

6X Ø10 THRU
ON PCD 90
PCD Ø90
Ø120
Ø45

A
A

Ø10
2 X 45°
Ø45
2 X 45°
20
20
R3
60
20
Ø45
PCD 90
120
SECTION A-A

EX-115

Ø120
6X Ø10
6X Ø8
PCD Ø90
Ø68
Ø45

A | | A

Ø120
Ø68
R2
Ø10
10
10
20
120
60
20
10
PCD 90

Ø120
PCD 90
Ø68
Ø45
Ø10
40
20
20
2 X 45°
R3
60
R3
Ø8
Ø55
Ø50
20
20
20
Ø45
Ø8

SECTION A-A

EX-116

120
100
10 | 25 | 50 | 25 | 10
4X Ø10
4X R5
25
A
A
30
50
15
25
10
Ø30
Ø20

20
80
50
R5
45
20
120

80
70
25
Ø10
30
R5
20
10
100
120

SECTION A-A

P-60

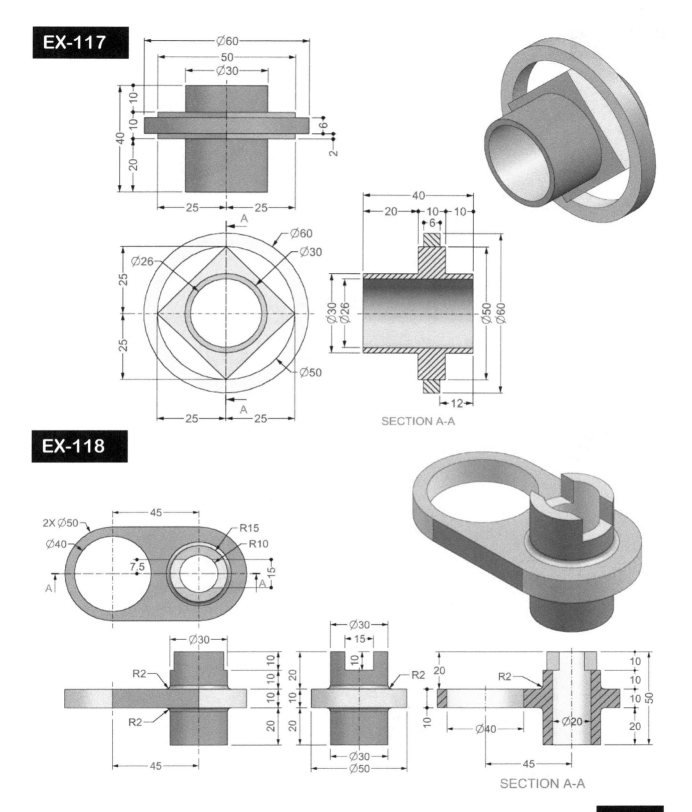

EX-117

Ø60
50
Ø30
40
10
10
20
6
2
25 25
A

Ø26
Ø60
Ø30
25
25
Ø50
25 25
A

40
20 10 10
6
Ø30
Ø26
Ø50
Ø60
12

SECTION A-A

EX-118

2X Ø50
Ø40
45
R15
R10
7.5
15
A
A

R2
Ø30
10 10
10 10
20
10 10
20
R2
20 20
45

Ø30
15
10
20
20
R2
10
Ø30
Ø50

20
R2
10
10
10
20
50
Ø40
Ø20
45

SECTION A-A

EX-119

Ø190
Ø55

Ø140
70
2X R20
2X R25
50
25
Ø55
Ø75
Ø100
Ø180
Ø190

SECTION A-A

A
50
25
R25
Ø75
Ø190

Ø75
Ø190
Ø55
Ø180
Ø100

EX-120

Ø50
Ø60
10
15
20
20
40
20
20
15
45
100

R15
A
Ø50
Ø70
Ø70
Ø40
Ø20
Ø30
Ø60
100
100

Ø50
Ø30
Ø60
Ø40
10
15
20
20
90
20
20
Ø20
15
40
45
100
100

SECTION A-A

P-62

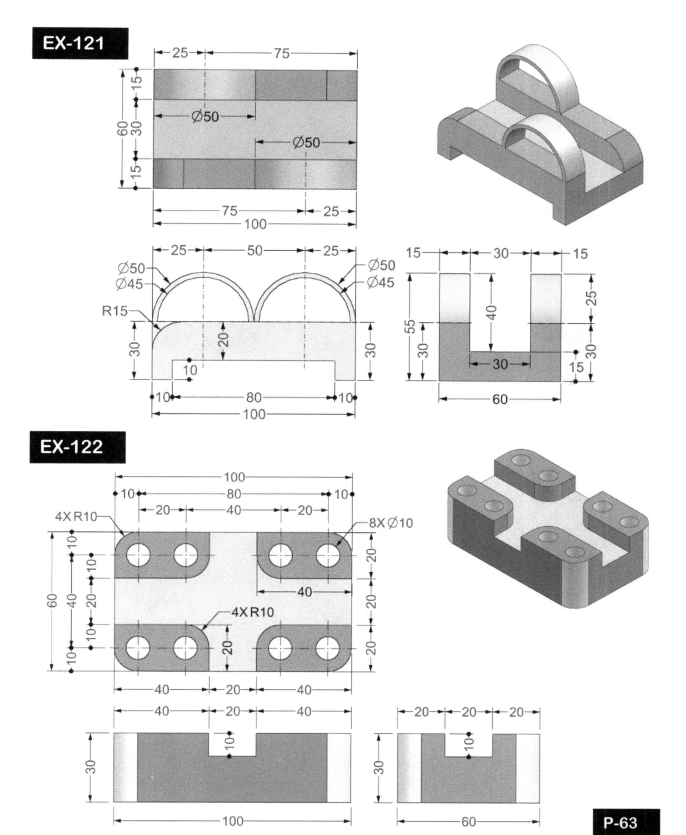

EX-121

EX-122

P-63

EX-123

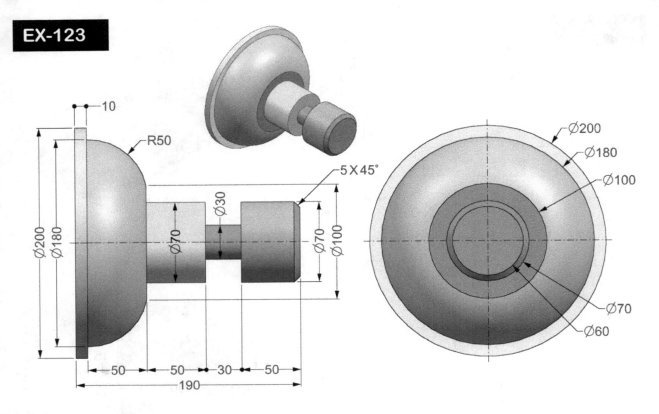

10
R50
5 X 45°
Ø30
Ø70
Ø70
Ø100
Ø200
Ø180
50 — 50 — 30 — 50
190

Ø200
Ø180
Ø100
Ø70
Ø60

EX-124

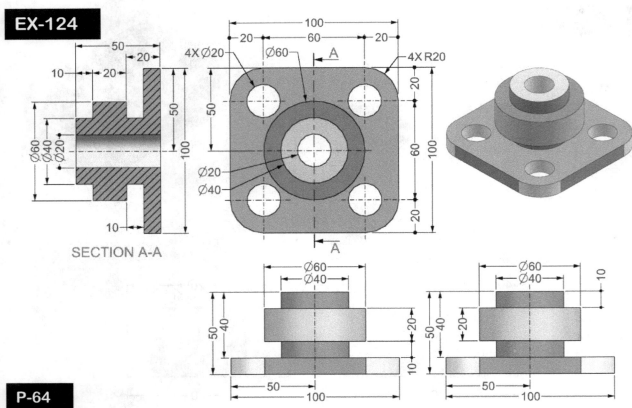

50
20
10
20
Ø60
Ø40
Ø20
50
100
10

SECTION A-A

100
20
60
20
4X Ø20
Ø60
A
4X R20
20
50
60
100
Ø20
Ø40
20
A

Ø60
Ø40
50
40
20
10
50
100

Ø60
Ø40
10
50
40
20
50
100

P-64

EX-125

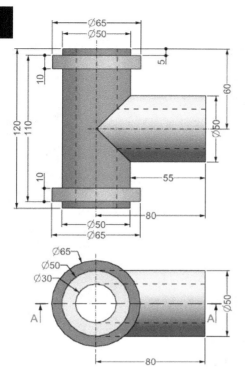

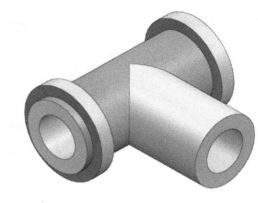

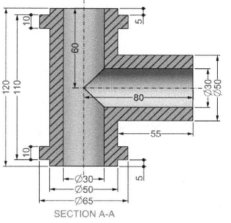

SECTION A-A

EX-126

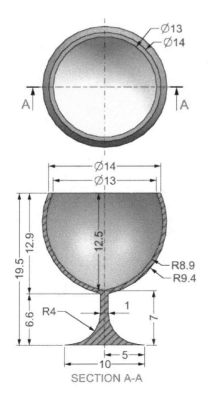

Ø14
Ø13

SECTION A-A

EX-127

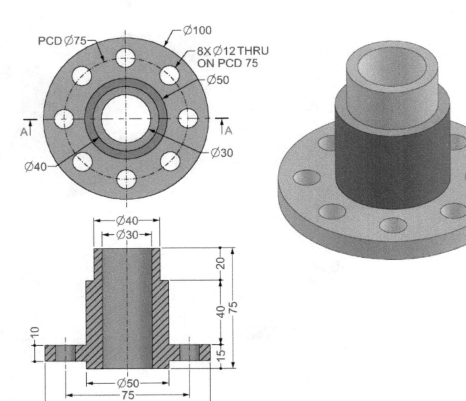

PCD Ø75
Ø100
8X Ø12 THRU
ON PCD 75
Ø50
Ø30
Ø40

A A

Ø40
Ø30
20
40
75
10
15
Ø50
75
Ø100

SECTION A-A

EX-128

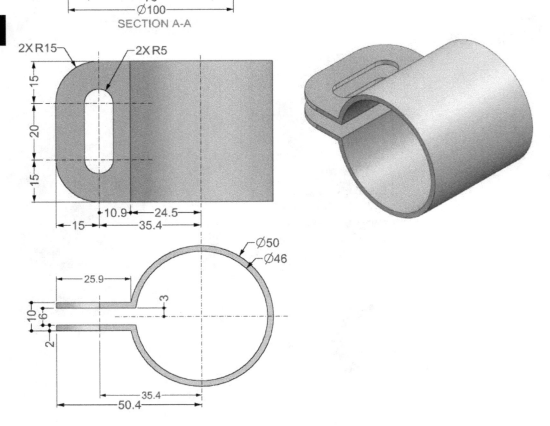

2X R15
2X R5

15
20
15

15
10.9
24.5
35.4

Ø50
Ø46

25.9
3
10
6
2
35.4
50.4

EX-129

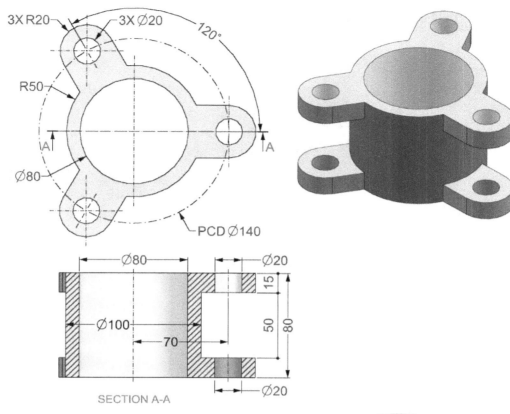

3X R20
3X Ø20
120°
R50
A
A
Ø80
PCD Ø140

Ø80
Ø20
15
Ø100
50
80
70
Ø20

SECTION A-A

EX-130

PCD Ø55
Ø70
A
A
8X Ø8
ON PCD 55
Ø30
Ø40

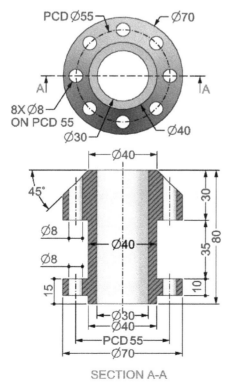

Ø40
45°
30
Ø8
Ø40
80
Ø8
35
15
10
Ø30
Ø40
PCD 55
Ø70

SECTION A-A

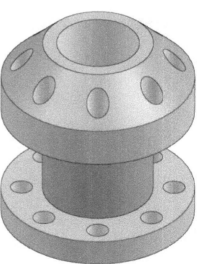

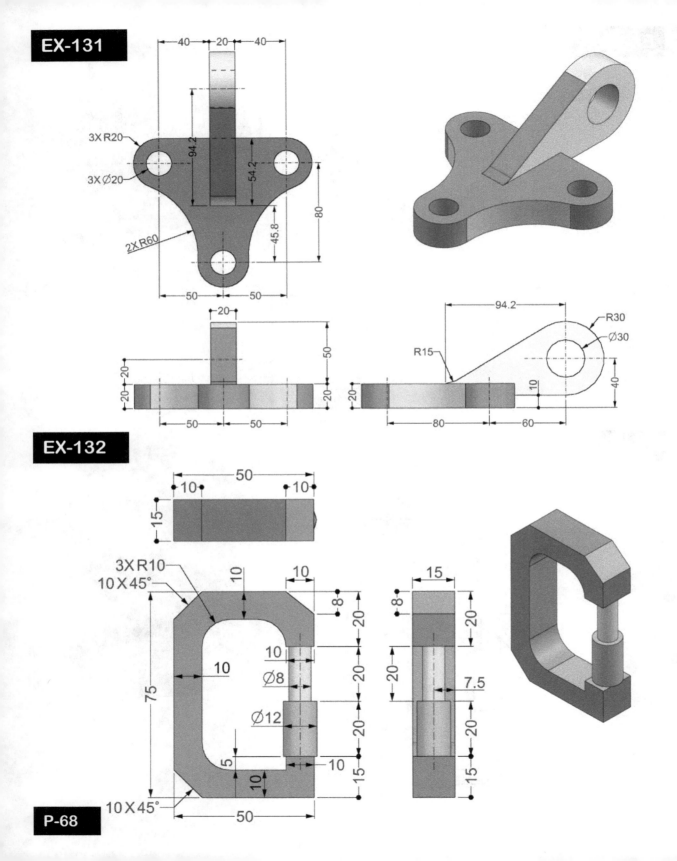

EX-131

3X R20
3X Ø20
2X R60

40 20 40
94.2
54.2
80
45.8
50 50

20
50
20 20 20
50 50

94.2
R30
Ø30
R15
20
10
40
80 60

EX-132

50
10 10
15

3X R10
10 X 45°
10
10
75
10
Ø8
10
Ø12
5
10
10 X 45°
50
20
8
20
20
20
15

15
8
20
20
7.5
20
15

P-68

EX-133

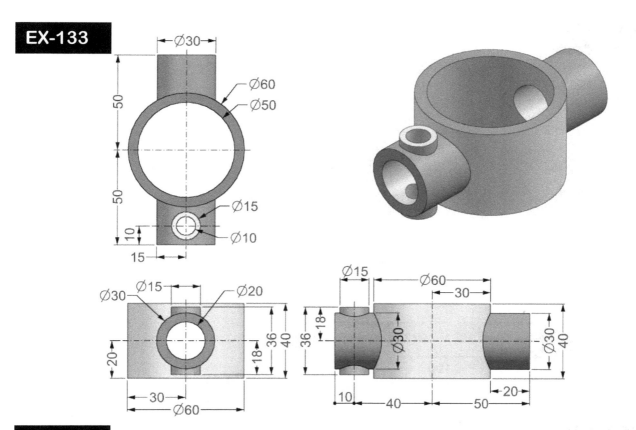

EX-134

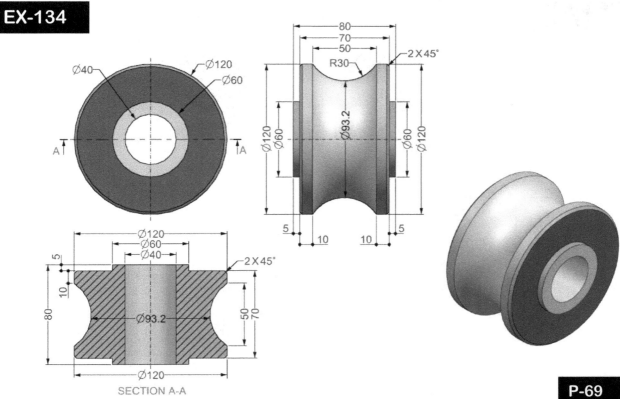

SECTION A-A

P-69

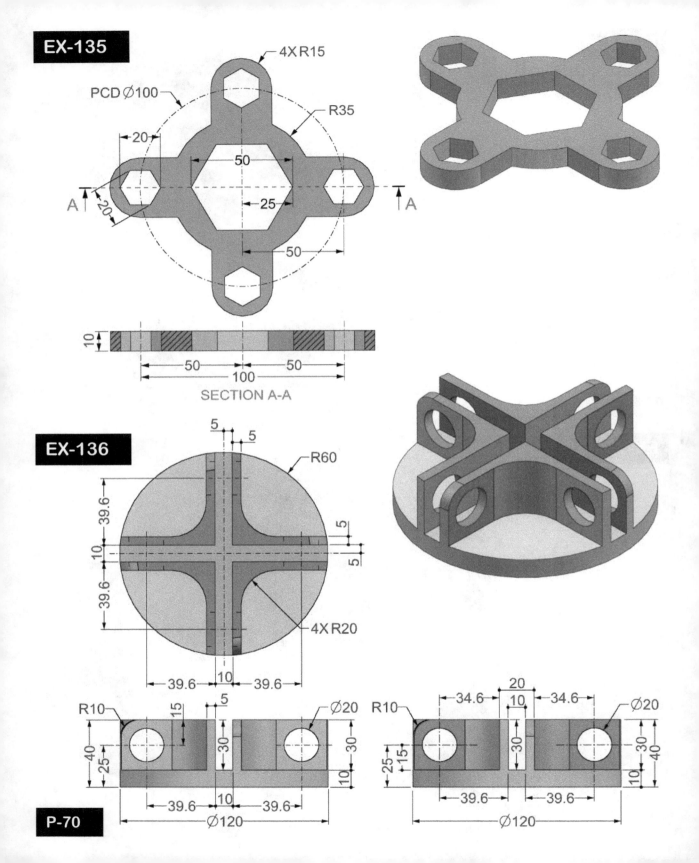

EX-135

PCD Ø100

4X R15

R35

20

50

25

50

20

A

A

SECTION A-A

10

50

50

100

EX-136

5

5

R60

39.6

39.6

10

5

5

39.6

39.6

4X R20

10

39.6

39.6

R10

15

5

Ø20

40

25

30

30

10

39.6

10

39.6

Ø120

R10

20

34.6

10

34.6

Ø20

25

15

30

30

40

10

39.6

39.6

Ø120

P-70

EX-137

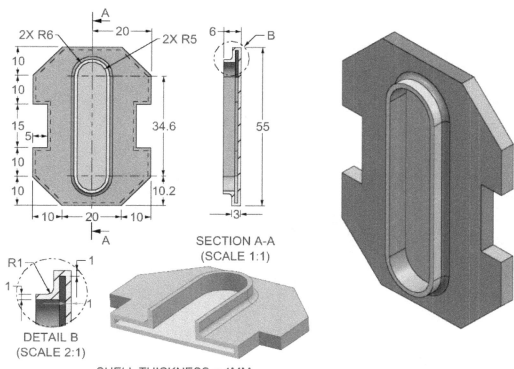

2X R6
2X R5
20
A
6
B

10
10
15
5
10
10

34.6
55

10.2
3

10
20
10

SECTION A-A
(SCALE 1:1)

R1
1
1
1

DETAIL B
(SCALE 2:1)

SHELL THICKNESS = 1MM
ALL INSIDE WALL THICKNESS

EX-138

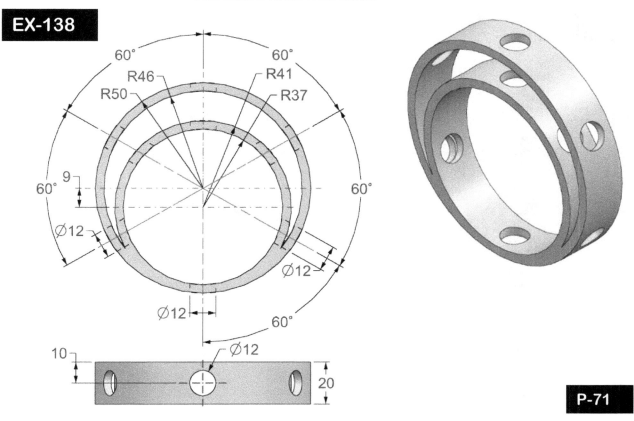

60°
60°
R46
R41
R50
R37
60°
9
60°
∅12
∅12
∅12
60°
∅12

10
20

EX-139

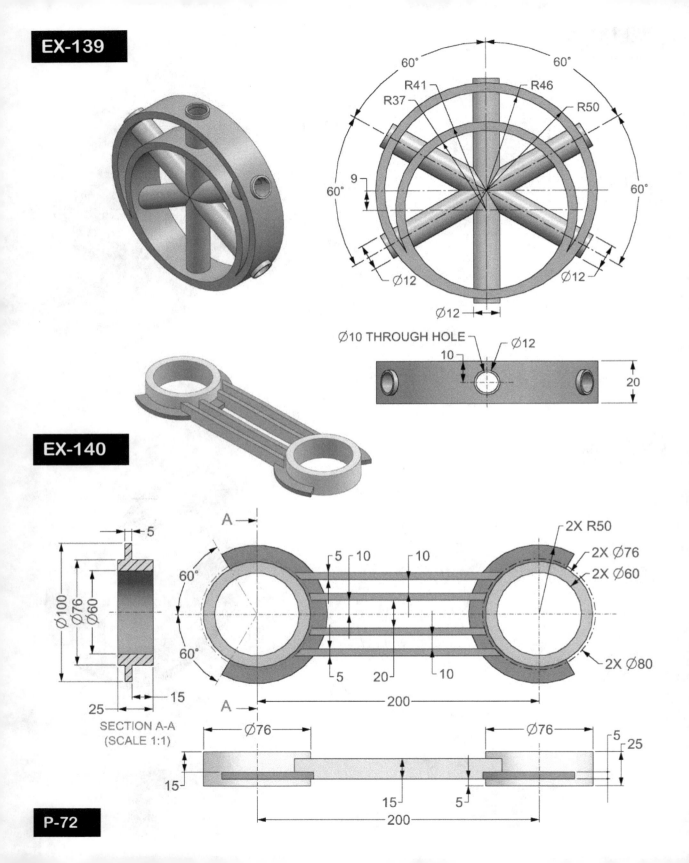

60°   60°
R41   R46
R37   R50
60°   60°
9
60°   60°
Ø12   Ø12
Ø12

Ø10 THROUGH HOLE   Ø12
10
20

EX-140

2X R50
2X Ø76
2X Ø60

5   10   10
60°
Ø100
Ø76
Ø60
60°
5
20   10

2X Ø80

5
15

25

SECTION A-A
(SCALE 1:1)

A
A

200

Ø76   Ø76
5
25
15
15   5
200

EX-141

Ø100
Ø60
Ø6
Ø120

Ø60
30 Ø6
R5
R40.7
10
10
100
50
Ø60
20
Ø80
R5
R2 R5
30
Ø120

EX-142

18 14 15 41.4
15.4
R15
R10
46.8 Ø16.2 Ø8
8
Ø20.4
23.4
26
Ø16.2
R6

10 20
15
5

P-73

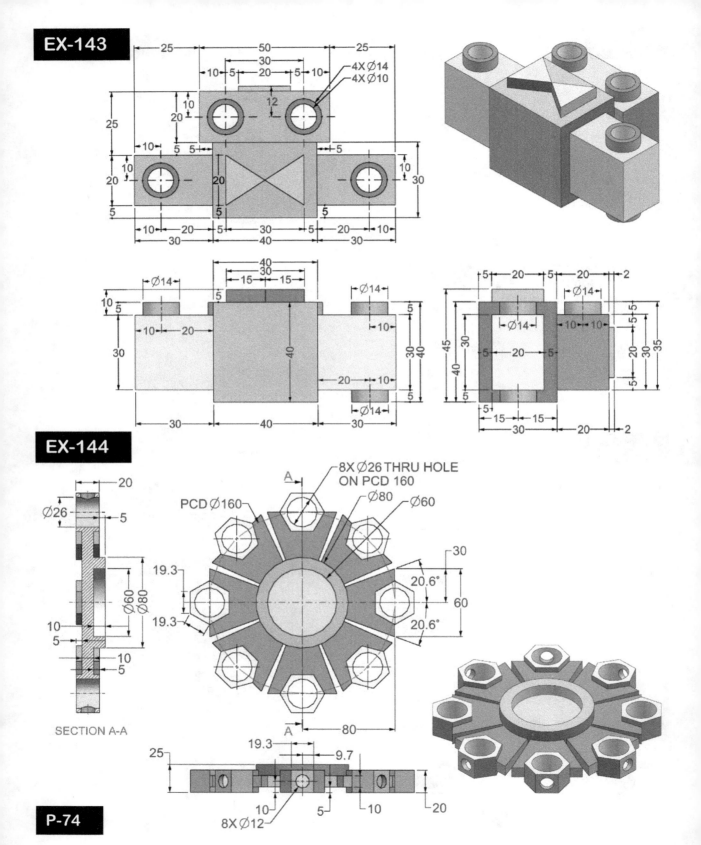

EX-143

4X Ø14
4X Ø10

EX-144

8X Ø26 THRU HOLE
ON PCD 160

PCD Ø160
Ø80
Ø60

SECTION A-A

8X Ø12

P-74

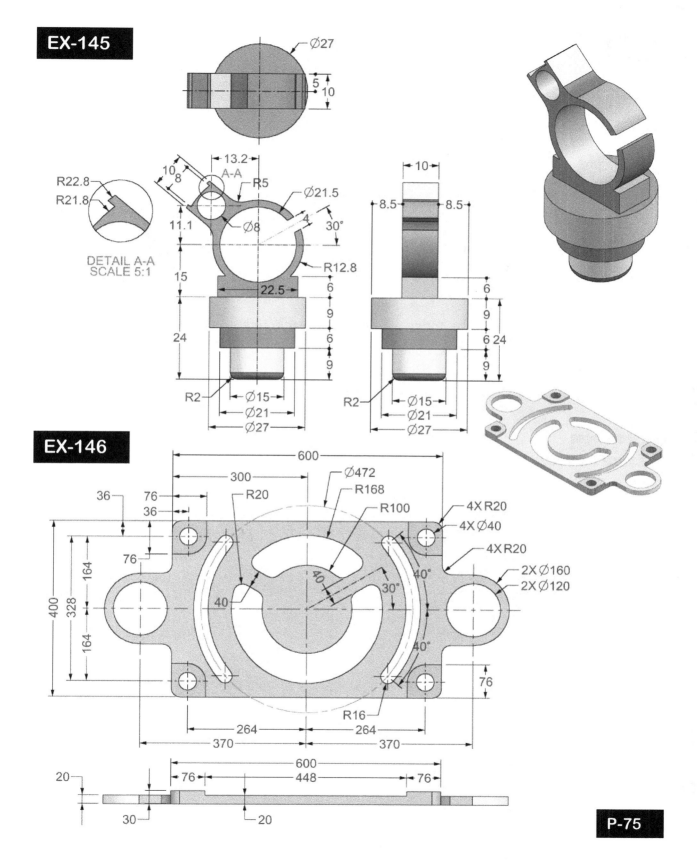

EX-145

∅27

5
10

13.2
A-A

10
8

R5

R22.8
R21.8

∅21.5

11.1

∅8

4

30°

DETAIL A-A
SCALE 5:1

15

R12.8

22.5

6

10

8.5   8.5

6

9

9

24

6

6   24

9

9

R2

∅15
∅21
∅27

R2

∅15
∅21
∅27

EX-146

600

300

∅472

R168

36

76

R20

R100

4X R20

36

4X ∅40

76

4X R20

164

40

40°

2X ∅160

400

328

30°

40°

2X ∅120

164

40

40°

76

264

264

R16

370

370

600

20

76

448

76

30

20

P-75

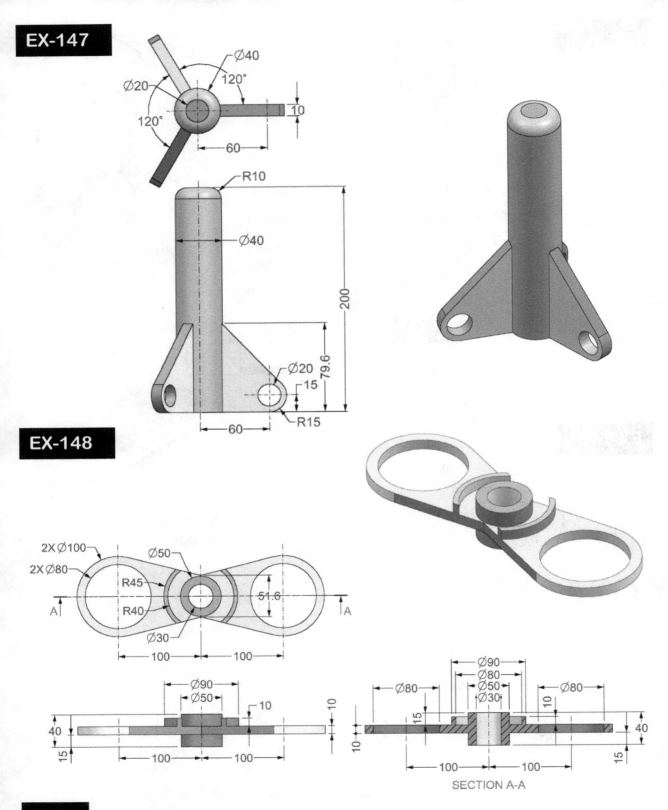

EX-147

∅40
120°
∅20
120°
10
60

R10
∅40
200
79.6
∅20
15
R15
60

EX-148

2X∅100
2X∅80
∅50
R45
R40
∅30
51.6
100
100

∅90
∅50
10
10
40
15
100
100

∅90
∅80
∅50
∅30
∅80
∅80
15
10
10
40
15
100
100
SECTION A-A

P-76

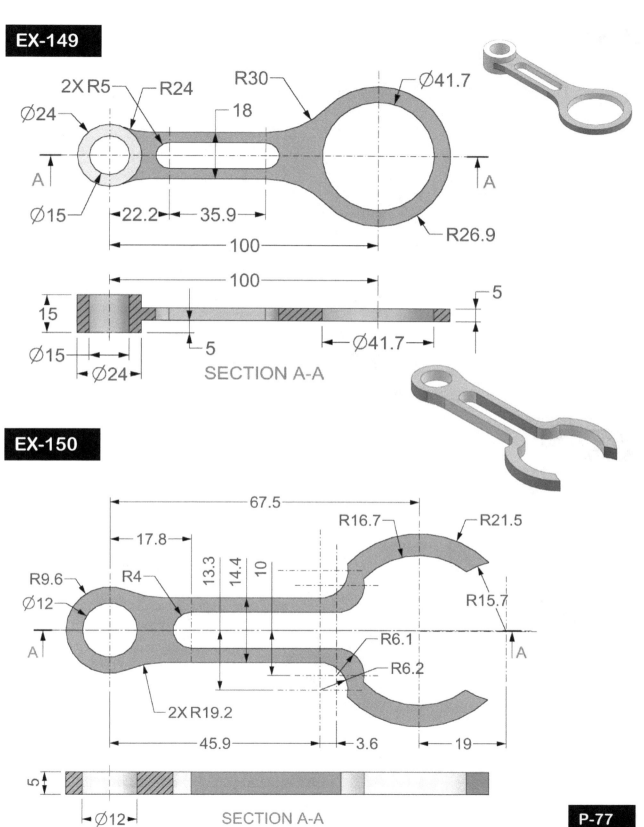

EX-149

2X R5 — R24
∅24
R30 — ∅41.7
18
A
A
∅15
22.2 — 35.9
100
R26.9

100
15
5
∅15
∅24
5
∅41.7
SECTION A-A

EX-150

67.5
17.8
13.3 14.4 10
R16.7 — R21.5
R9.6
R4
∅12
R15.7
A
A
R6.1
R6.2
2X R19.2
45.9
3.6
19

5
∅12
SECTION A-A

P-77

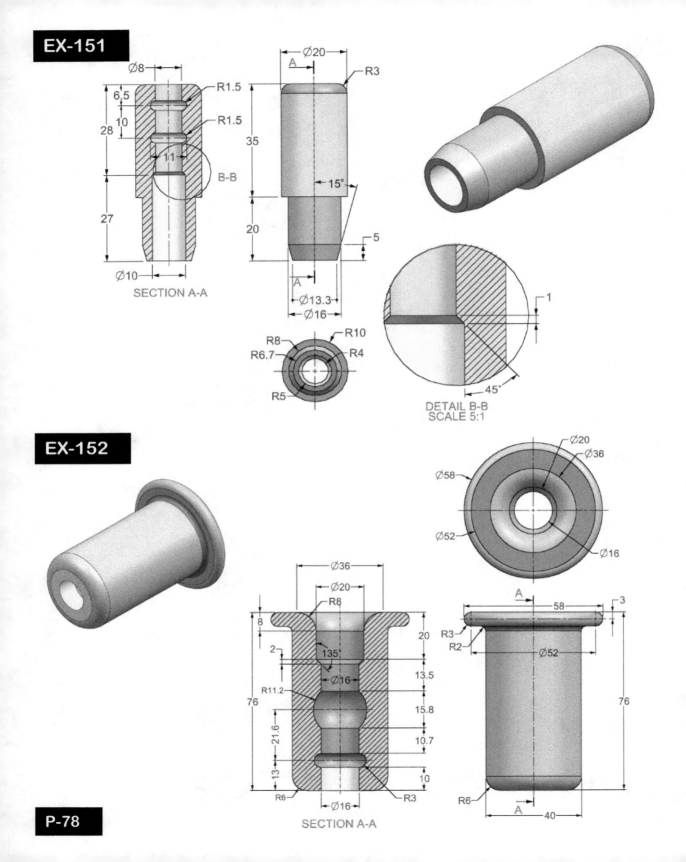

EX-151

Ø8

6.5
10
28
R1.5
R1.5
1:1
B-B
27
Ø10

SECTION A-A

Ø20
A
R3
35
15°
20
5
A
Ø13.3
Ø16

R8
R10
R6.7
R4
R5

1
45°

DETAIL B-B
SCALE 5:1

EX-152

Ø20
Ø36
Ø58
Ø52
Ø16

Ø36
Ø20
R8
8
2
135°
Ø16
20
13.5
R11.2
15.8
76
21.6
10.7
13
10
R6
Ø16
R3

SECTION A-A

A
58
3
R3
R2
Ø52
76
R6
A
40

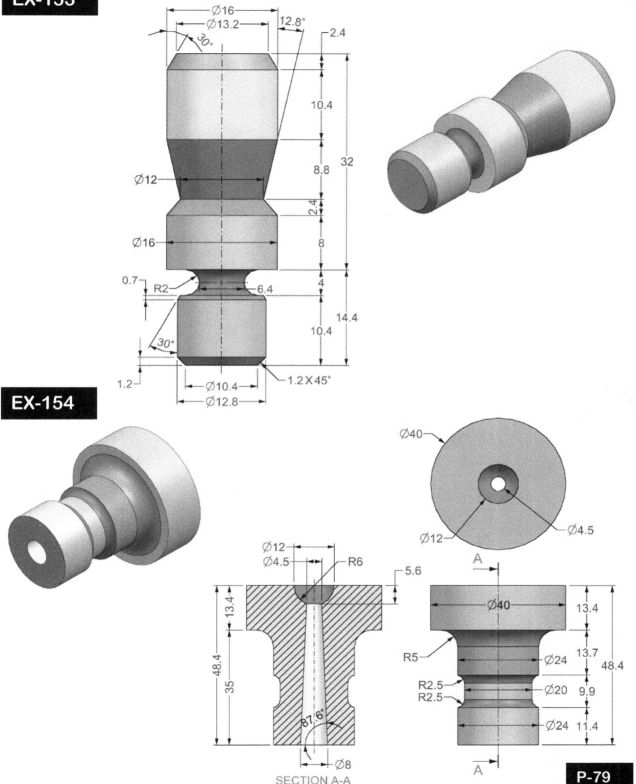

EX-153

EX-154

SECTION A-A

A

A

P-79

EX-155

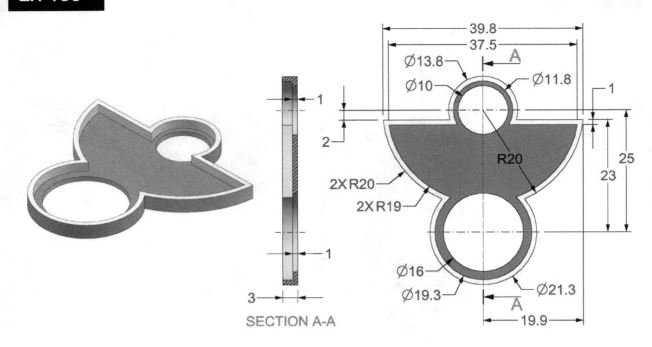

SECTION A-A

Ø13.8
Ø10
Ø11.8
39.8
37.5
A
R20
25
23
1
2
2X R20
2X R19
Ø16
Ø19.3
Ø21.3
A
19.9

EX-156

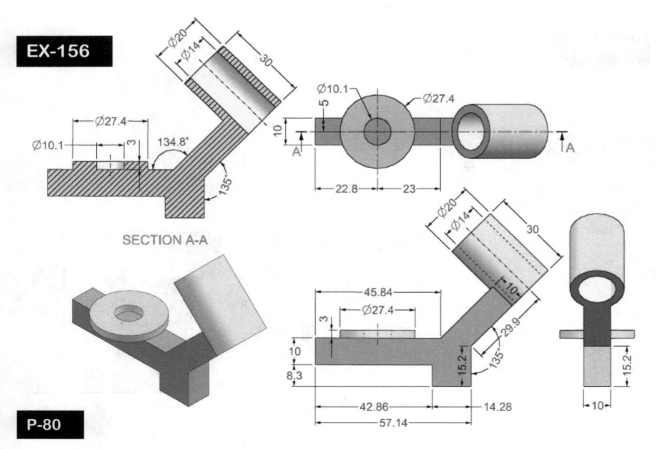

Ø20
Ø14
30
Ø27.4
Ø10.1
3
134.8°
135°
SECTION A-A

Ø10.1
Ø27.4
5
10
A
22.8
23
A

45.84
Ø27.4
3
10
8.3
42.86
14.28
57.14
135°
15.2
29.9
Ø20
Ø14
30
10
15.2
10

P-80

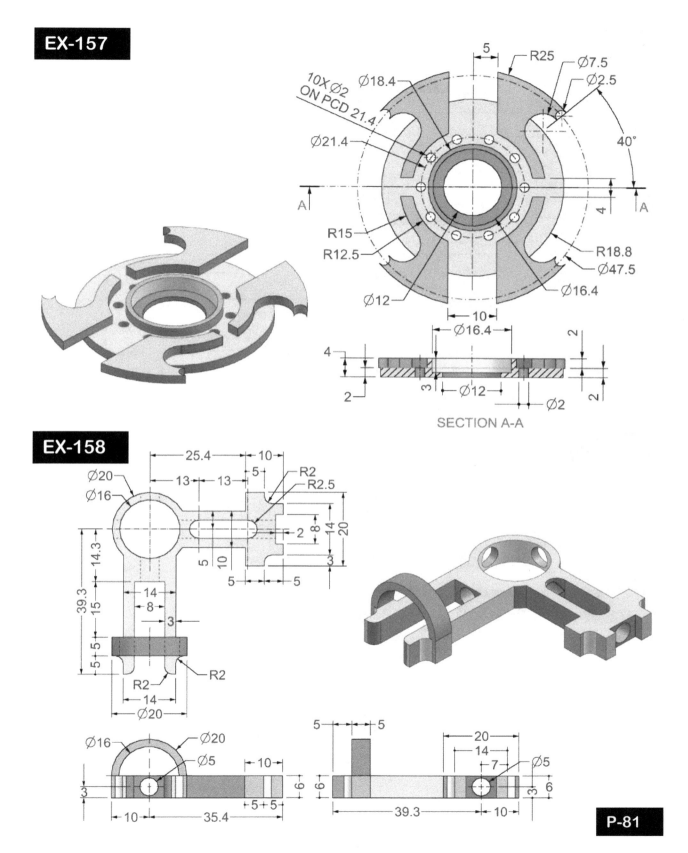

EX-157

10X Ø2
ON PCD 21.4
Ø18.4
5
R25
Ø7.5
Ø2.5
40°
Ø21.4
4
A
A
R15
R12.5
R18.8
Ø47.5
Ø12
Ø16.4
10
Ø16.4
4
2
2
3
Ø12
Ø2
2
SECTION A-A

EX-158

25.4
10
Ø20
Ø16
13
13
5
R2
R2.5
2
8
14
20
10
5
14.3
39.3
15
5
5
5
5
14
8
3
R2
R2
R2
14
Ø20
Ø16
Ø20
Ø5
10
3
5+5
10
35.4
6
5
5
20
14
7
Ø5
6
6
39.3
10
3

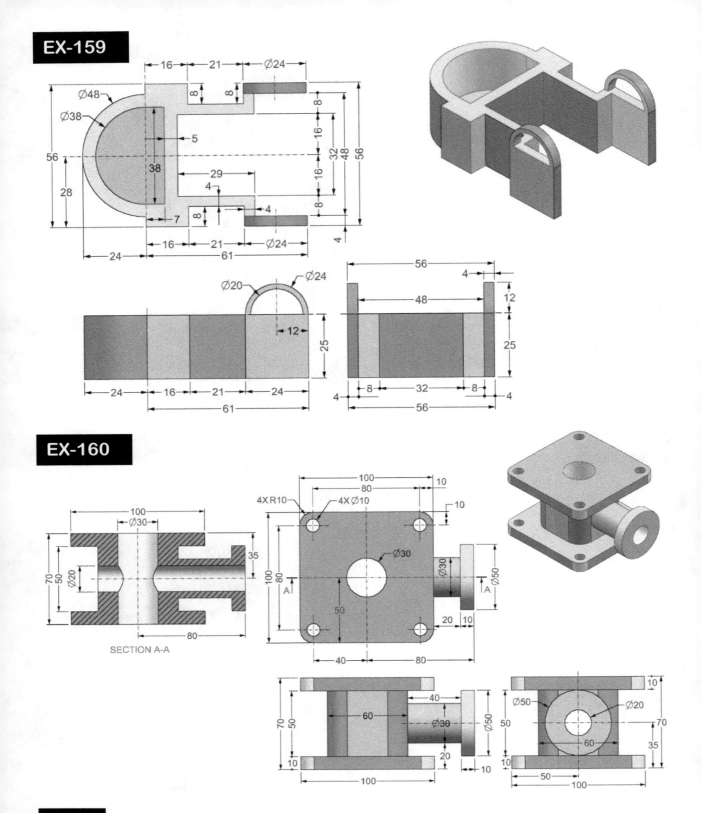

EX-159

EX-160

SECTION A-A

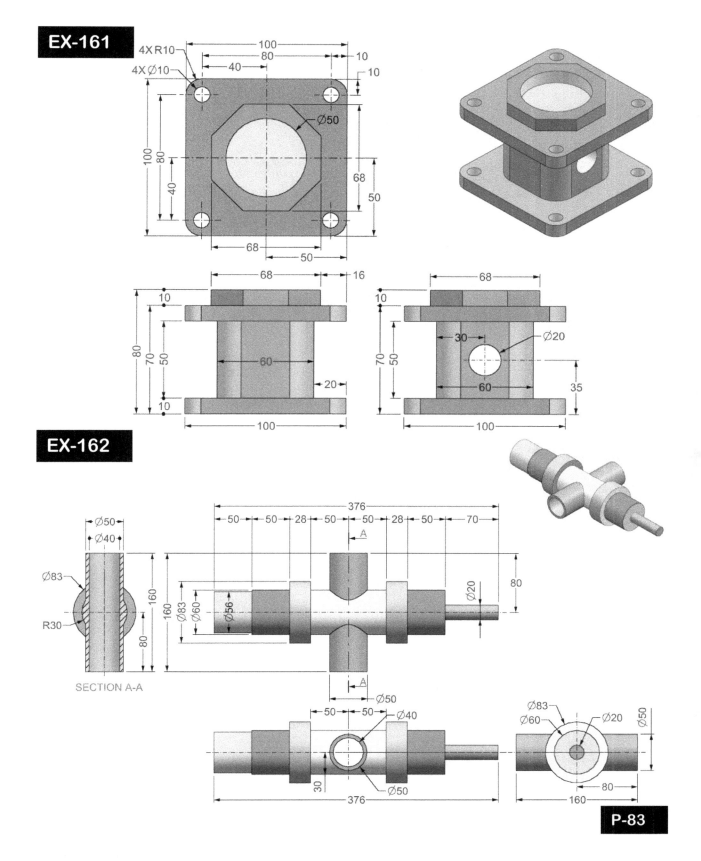

EX-161

4X R10
4X Ø10

100
80
40
10
10

Ø50

100 80 40

68 50

68 50

68 16
10
80 70 50
60
10
20

68
10
80 70 50
30 Ø20
60
35

100

100

EX-162

376
50 50 28 50 50 28 50 70
A

Ø50
Ø40

Ø83

R30

160
160
80

A

Ø83
Ø60
Ø56
Ø20

80

SECTION A-A

Ø50
50 50 Ø40

30
Ø50
376

Ø83
Ø60 Ø20

Ø50
80
160

P-83

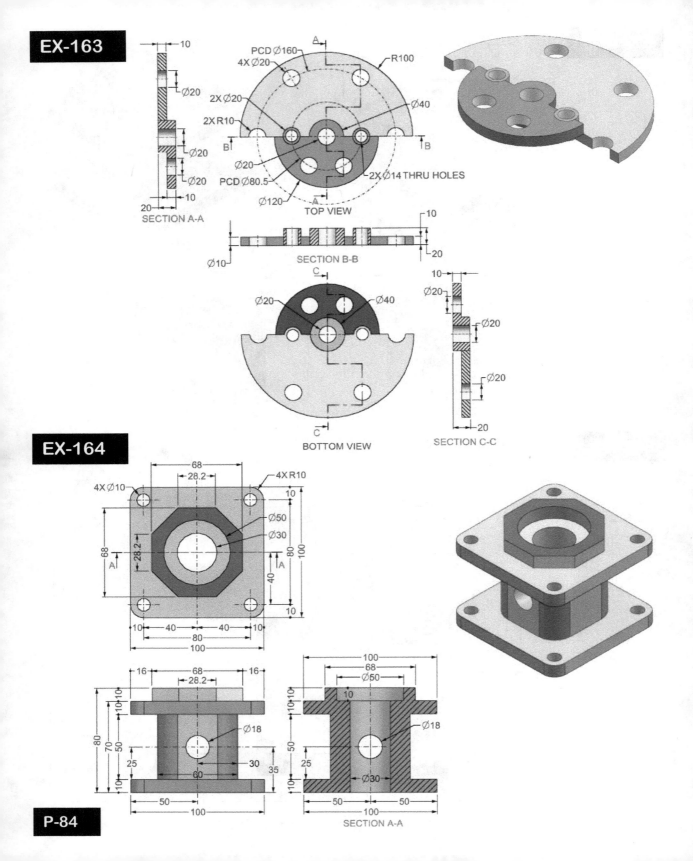

EX-163

PCD Ø160
4X Ø20
R100
2X Ø20
Ø40
2X R10
Ø20
PCD Ø80.5
2X Ø14 THRU HOLES
Ø120
TOP VIEW

10
Ø20
Ø20
Ø20
20
10
SECTION A-A
Ø10

10
20
SECTION B-B

Ø20
Ø40
BOTTOM VIEW

10
Ø20
Ø20
Ø20
20
SECTION C-C

EX-164

68
28.2
4X R10
4X Ø10
10
Ø50
Ø30
68
28.2
80
100
40
10
10
40
40
10
80
100
A
A

16
68
16
28.2
10
10
10
80
70
50
Ø18
25
30
10
60
35
50
100

100
68
Ø50
10
10
10
Ø18
50
25
10
Ø30
50
50
100
SECTION A-A

P-84

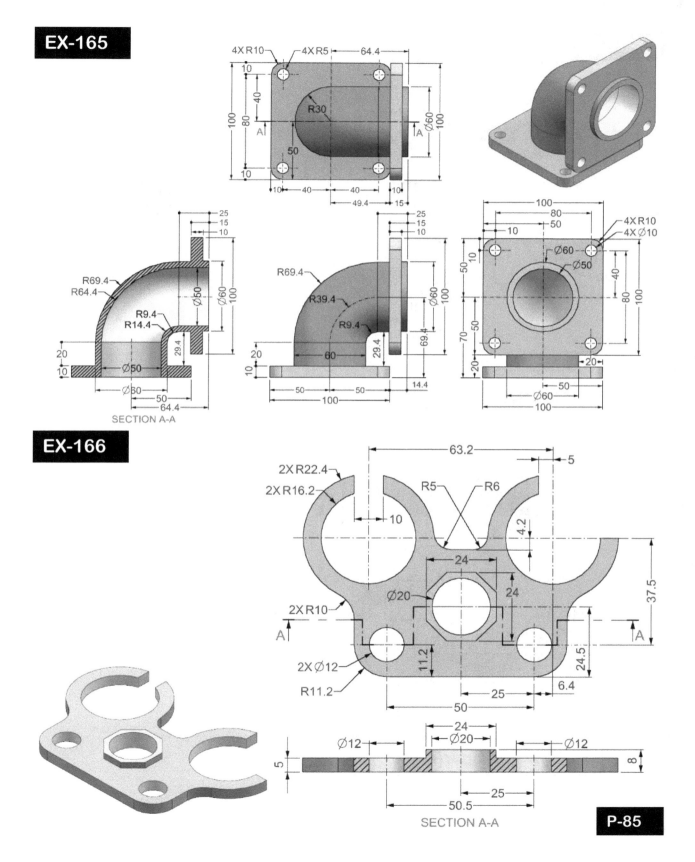

EX-165

SECTION A-A

EX-166

SECTION A-A

P-85

EX-167

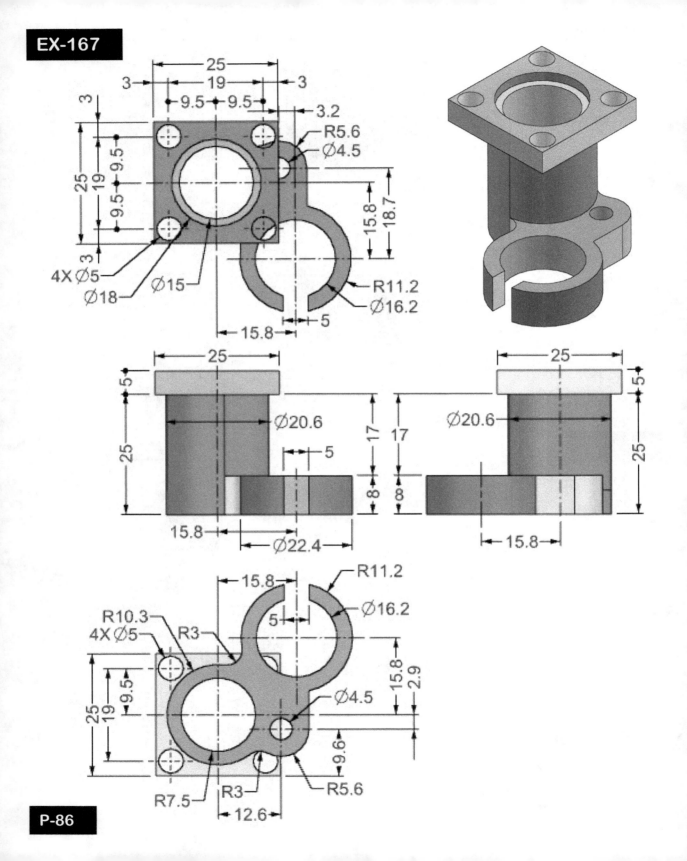

P-86

EX-165

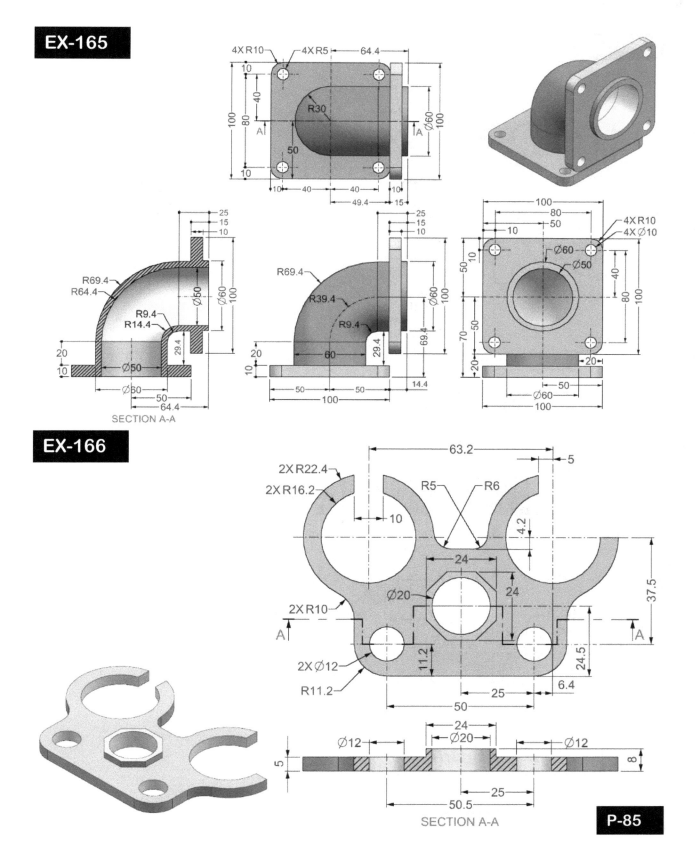

SECTION A-A

EX-166

SECTION A-A

P-85

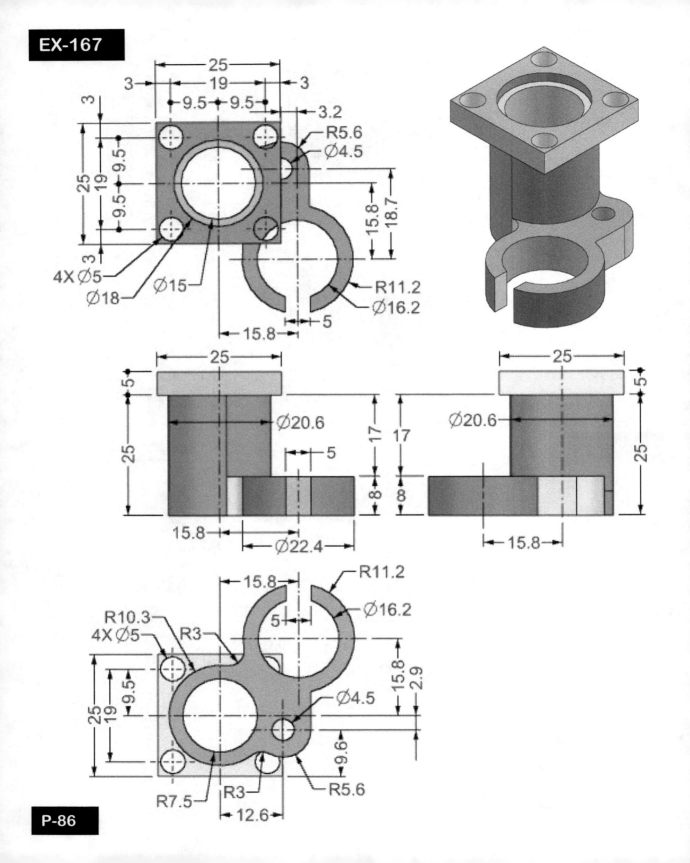

EX-167

P-86

EX-168

PCD Ø95
Ø120
8X Ø14
8X Ø10
ON PCD 95
R35
R25

A
A

6
3

32
30
80 16
32

20
2

Ø70
Ø120

30

Ø14
Ø10

16 20

Ø50
Ø70
PCD 95
Ø120

SECTION A-A

EX-169

Ø70
Ø40

20
40

R5
Ø28
Ø40

50
130
70
200

Ø70
R2
R60
Ø80
R5

30
21.3
40
50
80
140
Ø28
Ø40

10

50
80
70

Ø70
15 40 15
10

30
Ø28
Ø40
80

15
15
70

30
10

35
Ø70

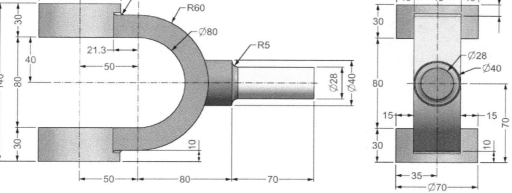

P-87

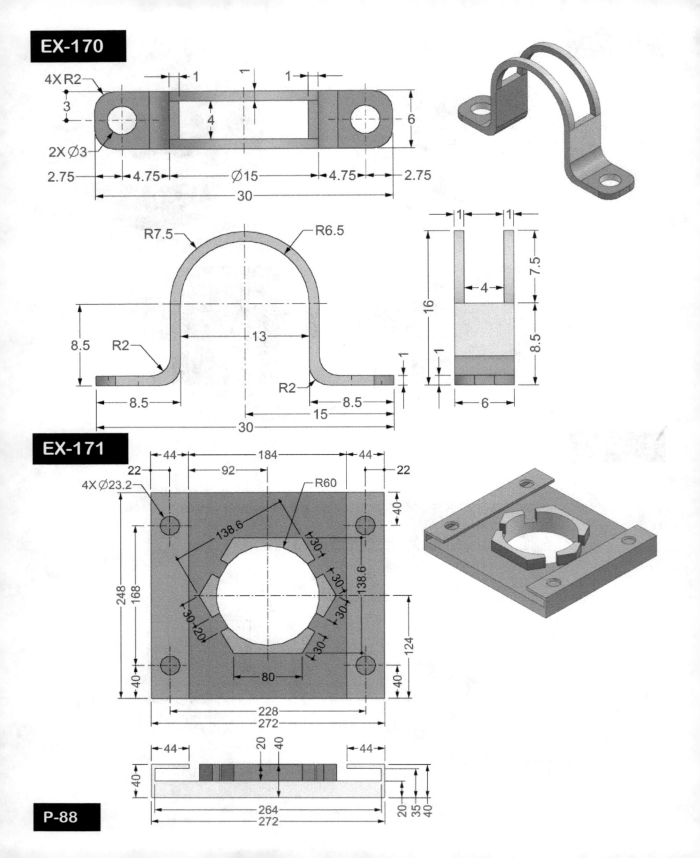

EX-170

4X R2
3
2X Ø3
2.75 — 4.75 — Ø15 — 4.75 — 2.75
30
1
1
1
4
6

R7.5
R6.5
R2
13
8.5
R2
8.5
15
8.5
30

1
1
7.5
4
16
1
8.5
6

EX-171

44
184
44
22
22
4X Ø23.2
R60
92
138.6
30
30
138.6
40
138.6
30
30
168
248
30
20
30
124
80
40
40
228
272

44
20
40
44
40
20
35
40
264
272

P-88

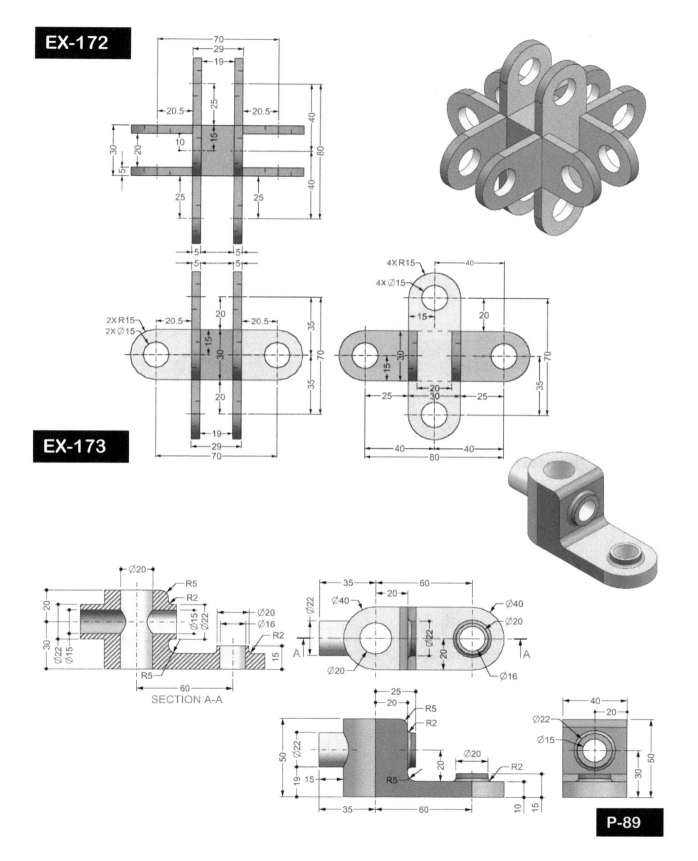

EX-172

EX-173

2X R15
2X Ø15

4X R15
4X Ø15

SECTION A-A

P-89

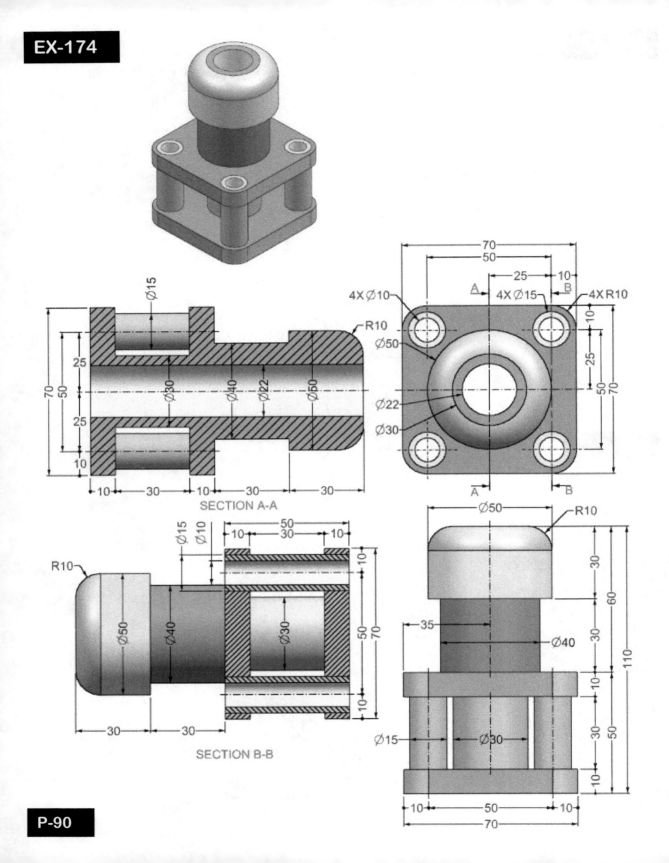

EX-174

SECTION A-A

SECTION B-B

P-90

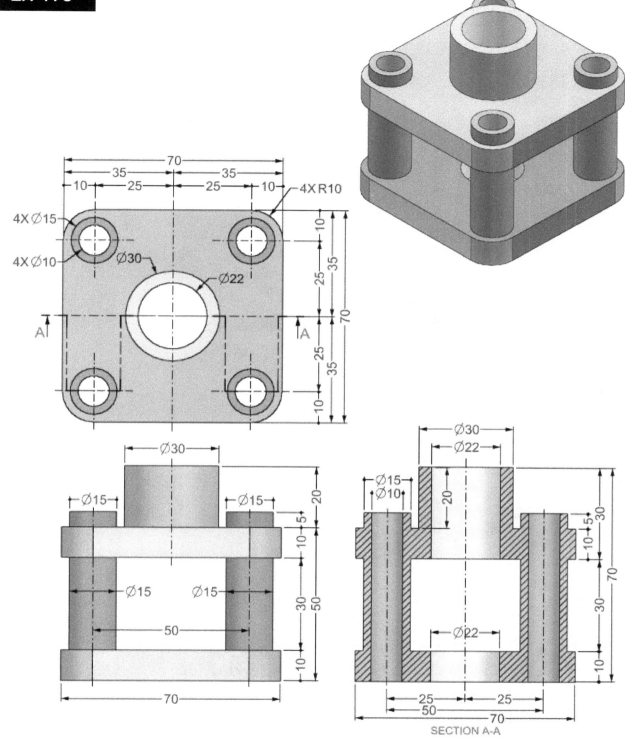

SECTION A-A

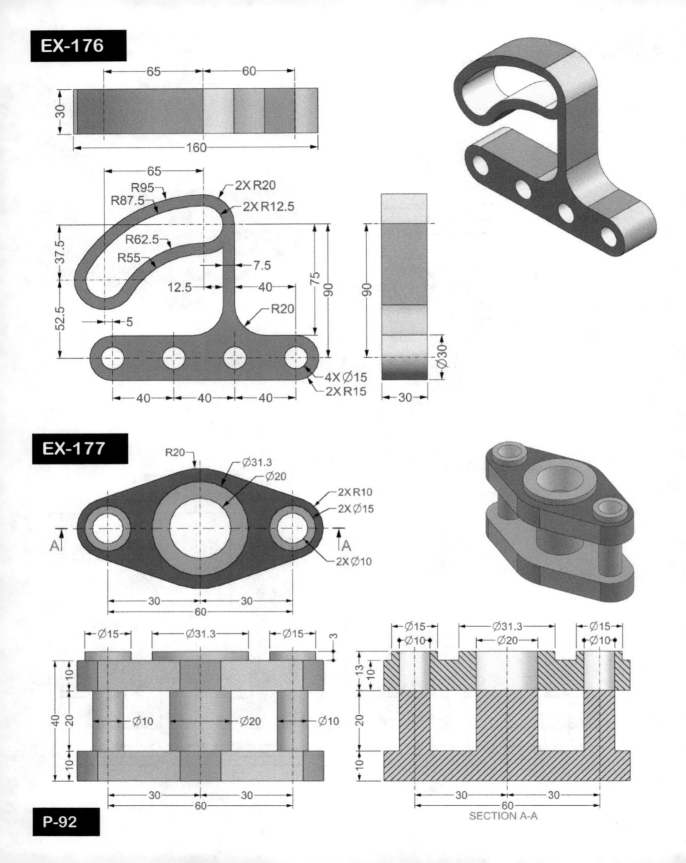

EX-176

65 · 60
30
160

65
R95
R87.5
2X R20
2X R12.5
R62.5
R55
37.5
7.5
12.5 · 40
75
90
90
52.5
R20
5
Ø30
4X Ø15
40 · 40 · 40
2X R15
30

EX-177

R20
Ø31.3
Ø20
2X R10
2X Ø15
A
A
2X Ø10
30 · 30
60

Ø15
Ø31.3
Ø15
3
10
Ø15
Ø31.3
Ø15
Ø10
Ø20
Ø10
40
20
13
10
Ø10
Ø20
Ø10
20
10
10
30 · 30
30 · 30
60
60
SECTION A-A

P-92

EX-178

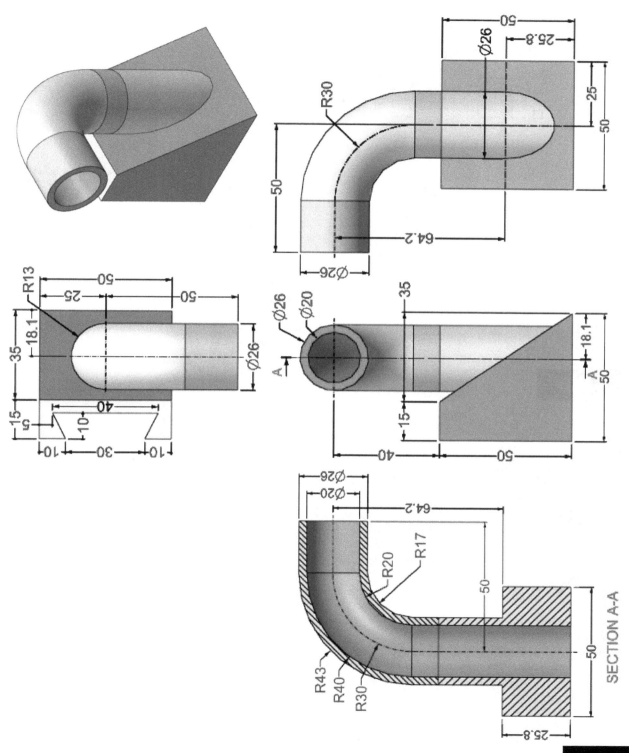

R30
Ø26
50
25.8
25
50
64.2
Ø26

R13
50
25
50
35
18.1
Ø26
40
15
5
10
10
30

Ø26
Ø20
A
35
18.1
A
50
15
40
50

Ø26
Ø20
64.2
R20
R17
50
R43
R40
R30
50
25.8

SECTION A-A

P-93

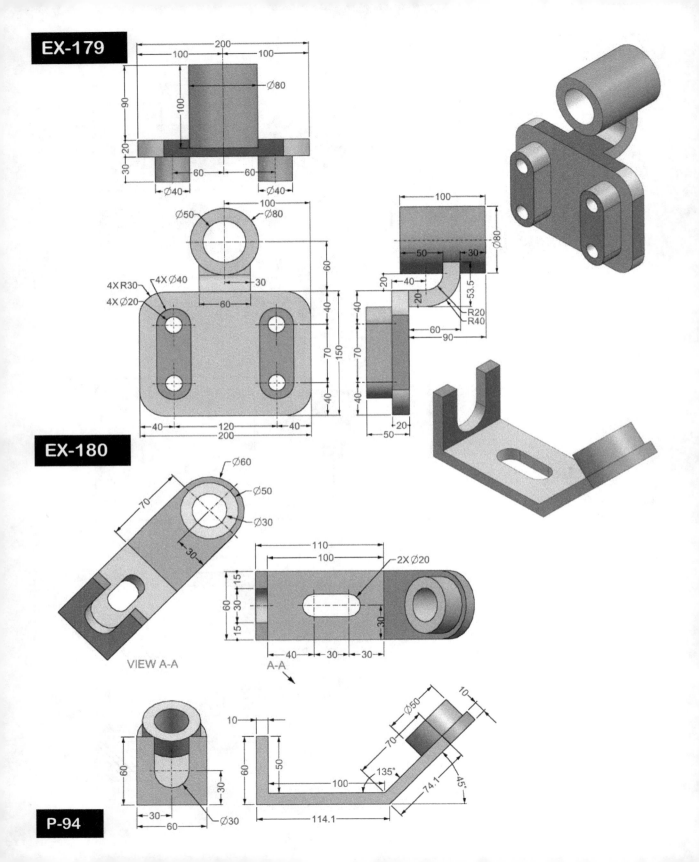

EX-179

EX-180

VIEW A-A

A-A

P-94

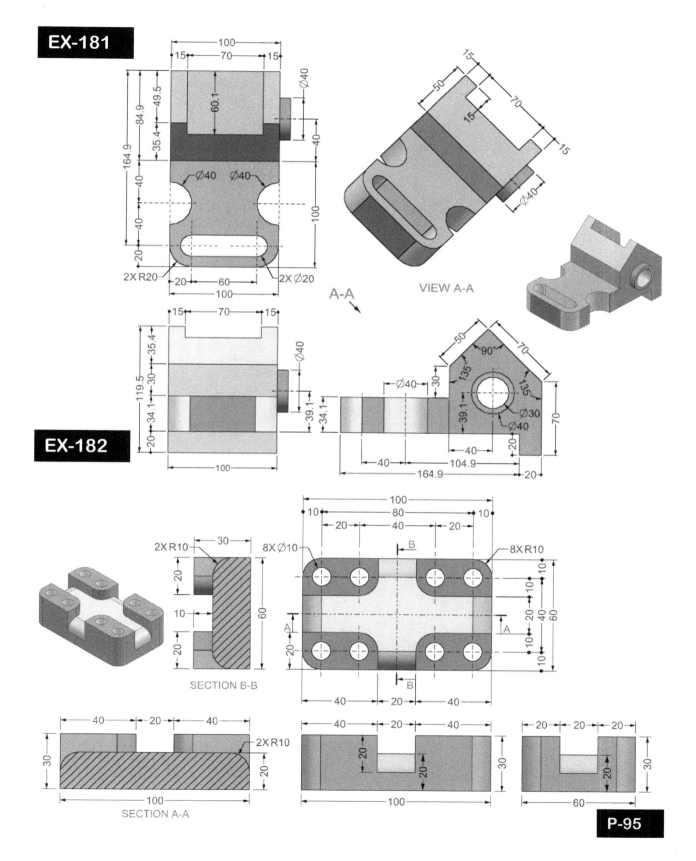

EX-181

Ø40

VIEW A-A

A-A

EX-182

2X R20   2X Ø20

2X R10   8X Ø10   8X R10

B

A   A

B

SECTION B-B

SECTION A-A

2X R10

P-95

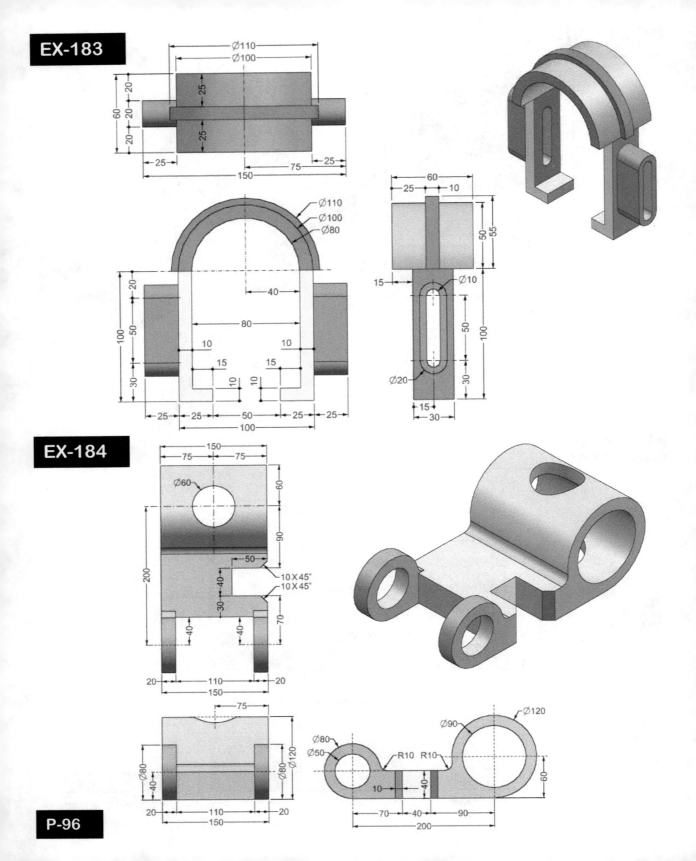

EX-183

EX-184

P-96

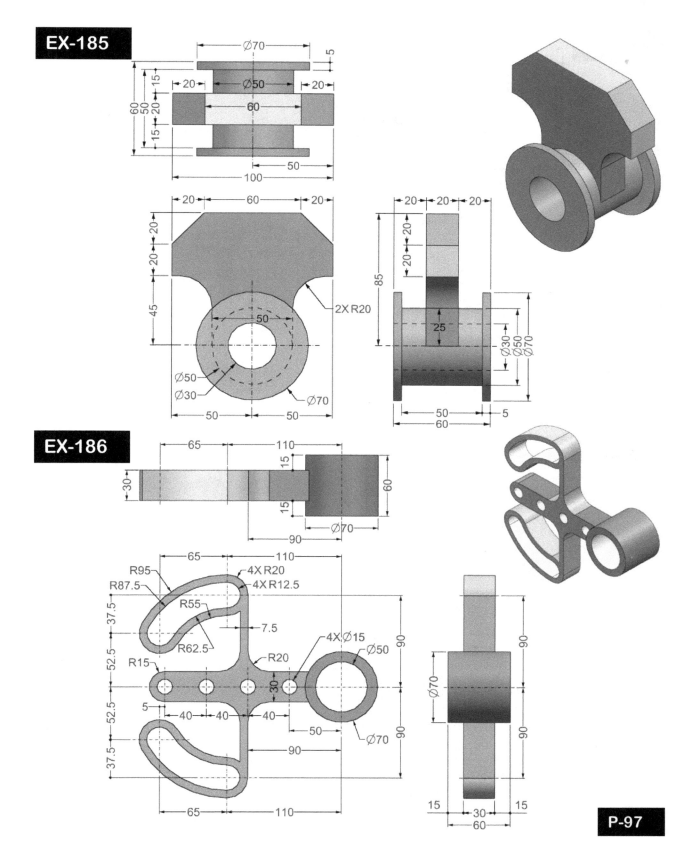

EX-185

⌀70
5
20
15
60
50
20
⌀50
60
20
15
50
100

20
60
20
20
20
45
50
2X R20
⌀50
⌀30
⌀70
50
50

20
20
20
20
20
85
25
⌀30
⌀50
⌀70
50
5
60

EX-186

65
110
30
15
60
15
90
⌀70

65
110
R95
4X R20
R87.5
4X R12.5
37.5
R55
7.5
R62.5
52.5
4X⌀15
⌀50
R15
R20
30
52.5
5
40
40
40
50
⌀70
37.5
90
⌀70
90
90
⌀70
90
15
30
15
60
65
110

P-97

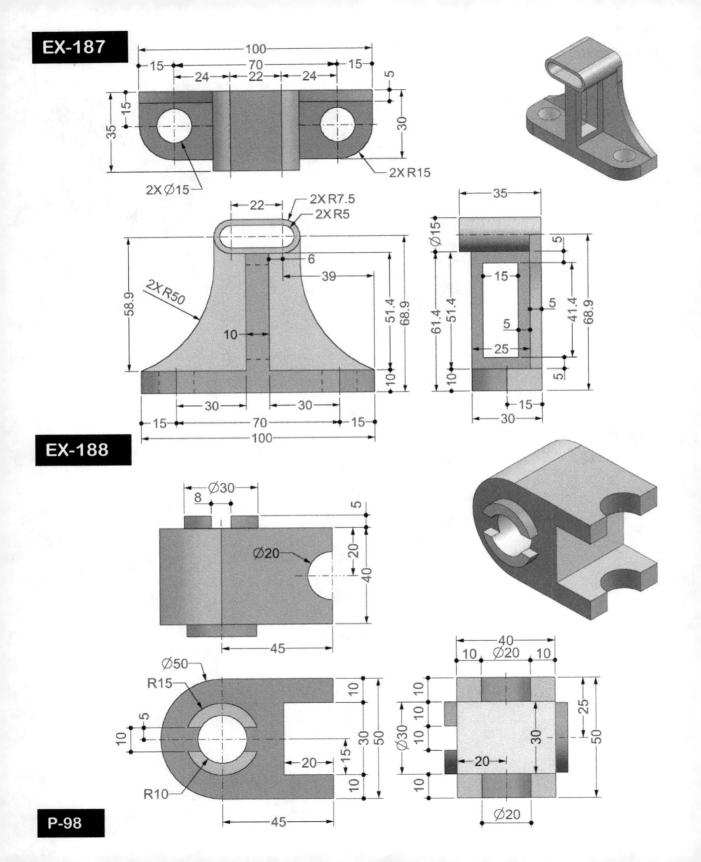

EX-187

100
15
70
15
24 22 24
5
35
15
30
2X⌀15
2X R15

22
2X R7.5
2X R5
6
39
58.9
2X R50
51.4
68.9
10
10
30 30
15 70 15
100

35
⌀15
5
61.4
51.4
15
5
5
41.4
68.9
25
10
5
15
30

EX-188

⌀30
8
5
⌀20
20
40
45

⌀50
R15
10
10
5
R10
20
30
15
10
50
45

40
10 ⌀20 10
10
⌀30
10
10
25
30
50
20
10
⌀20

P-98

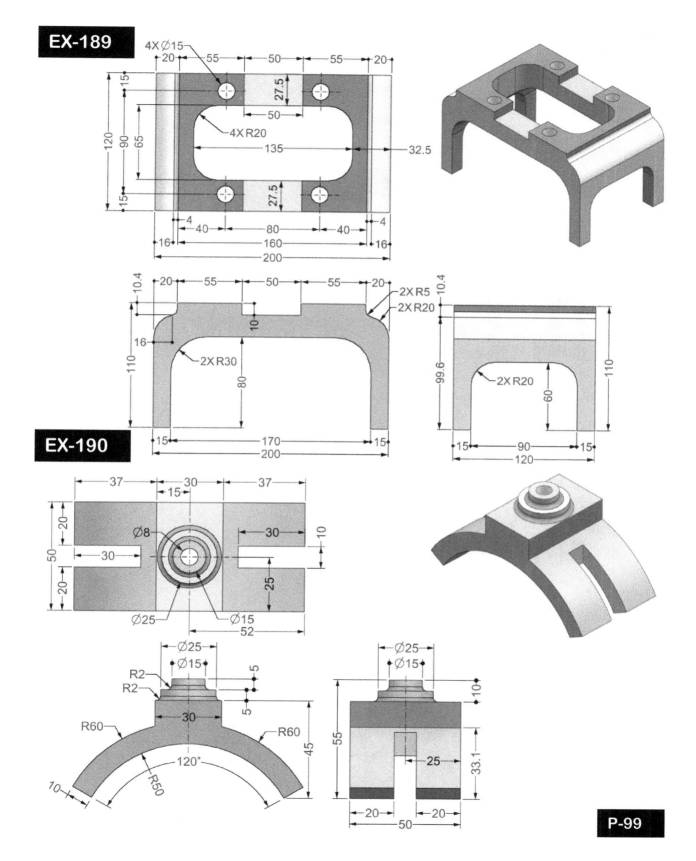

EX-189

4X Ø15
20 · 55 · 50 · 55 · 20
15
120
90
65
27.5
50
4X R20
135 · 32.5
15
27.5
4
40 · 80 · 40
4
16 · 160 · 16
200

10.4
20 · 55 · 50 · 55 · 20
2X R5
2X R20
16
10
110
2X R30
80
15 · 170 · 15
200

EX-190

10.4
99.6
2X R20
110
60
15 · 90 · 15
120

37 · 30 · 37
15
20
50
20
Ø8
30
30
10
25
Ø25 · Ø15
52

Ø25
Ø15
R2
R2
5
5
30
R60
R60
45
120°
R50
10

Ø25
Ø15
10
55
33.1
25
20 · 20
50

P-99

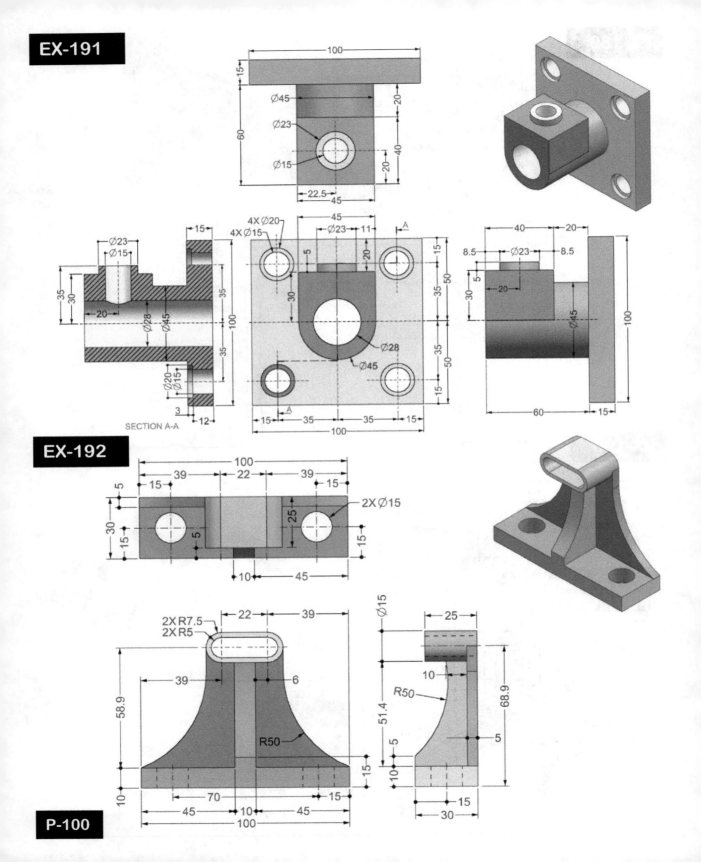

EX-191

Ø45
Ø23
Ø15

SECTION A-A

4X Ø20
4X Ø15
Ø23

Ø28
Ø45

EX-192

2X Ø15

P-100

2X R7.5
2X R5

R50

Ø15

R50

EX-193

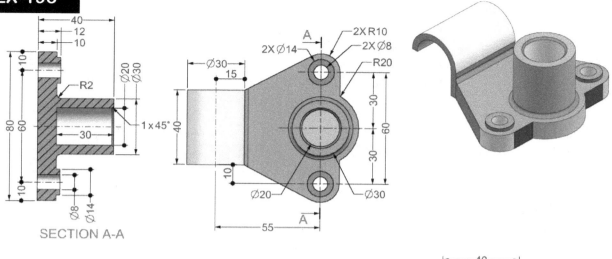

SECTION A-A

2X R10
2X Ø14
2X Ø8
R20
Ø30
15
40
Ø30
30
60
30
10
Ø20
Ø30
55

Ø30
Ø20
Ø30
30
30
R2
80
60
10
10
1 x 45°
Ø8
Ø14
40
12
10

Ø30
Ø23
R2
R2
Ø30
Ø14
40
15
55
10
12

40
Ø30
Ø14
20
R3.2
40
10
12
30
30
60

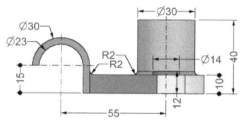
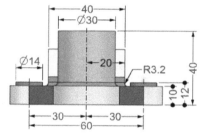

EX-194

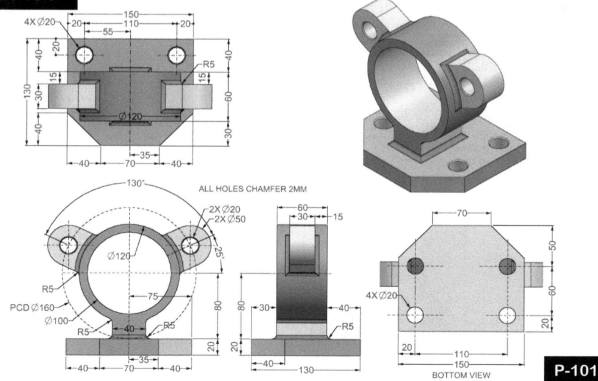

4X Ø20
150
110
20
20
55
40
20
R5
15
130
30
15
60
Ø120
40
30
40
70
35
40

130°
2X Ø20
2X Ø50
25°
Ø120
R5
75
80
PCD Ø160
Ø100
R5
R5
40
40
70
40
35
20

ALL HOLES CHAMFER 2MM

60
30
15
80
30
40
20
R5
40
130

70
50
60
Ø14
4X Ø20
20
20
110
BOTTOM VIEW

P-101

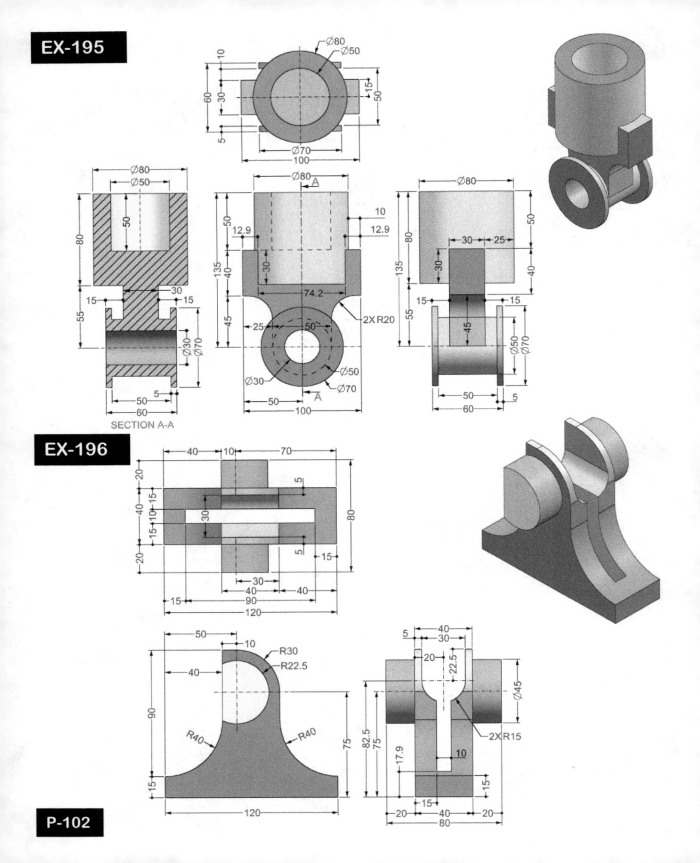

EX-195

Ø80
Ø50
10
60
30
50
15
5
Ø70
100

Ø80
Ø50
80
50
30
15
15
55
5
50
60
SECTION A-A
Ø30
Ø70

Ø80
A
50
12.9
135
40
30
10
12.9
74.2
2X R20
45
25
50
Ø30
Ø50
Ø70
50
100
A

Ø80
80
50
30
135
30
25
55
15
15
45
Ø50
Ø70
50
60
5

EX-196

40
10
70
20
40
15 10 15
15 10
30
5
80
5
15
20
15
30
40
90
120
40

50
10
R30
R22.5
40
90
R40
R40
75
15
120

40
30
5
20
22.5
Ø45
82.5
75
2X R15
17.9
10
15
15
20
40
20
80

P-102

EX-197

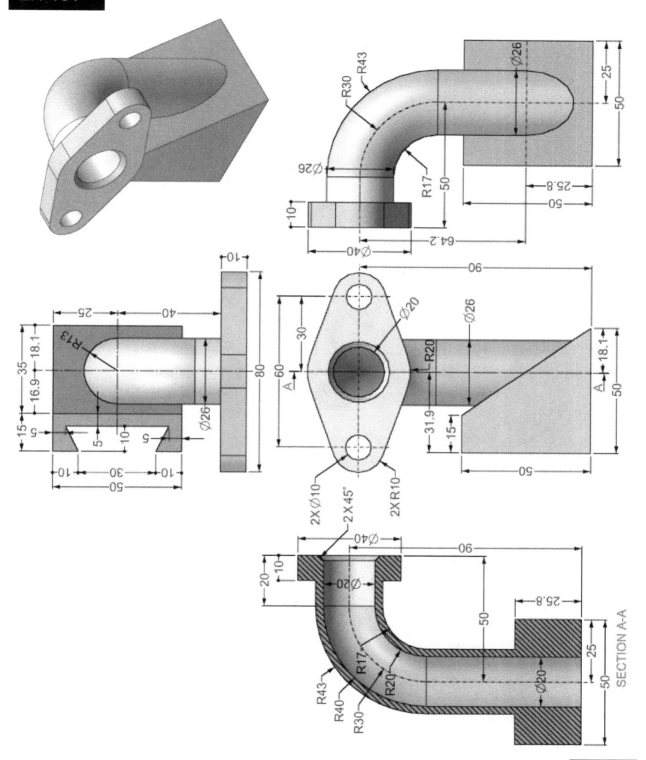

SECTION A-A

P-103

EX-198

6X Ø15 THRU
ON PCD 90

Ø120
Ø50
Ø40

PCD Ø90

A

A

Ø20

VIEW B-B

8X Ø10 THRU
ON PCD 54

Ø30
Ø70

PCD Ø54

B-B

SECTION A-A

Ø120
Ø50
Ø40

15

10

Ø15

120

30

60°
60°

80

Ø10

5

10

Ø20
Ø30
PCD 54

P-104

EX-199

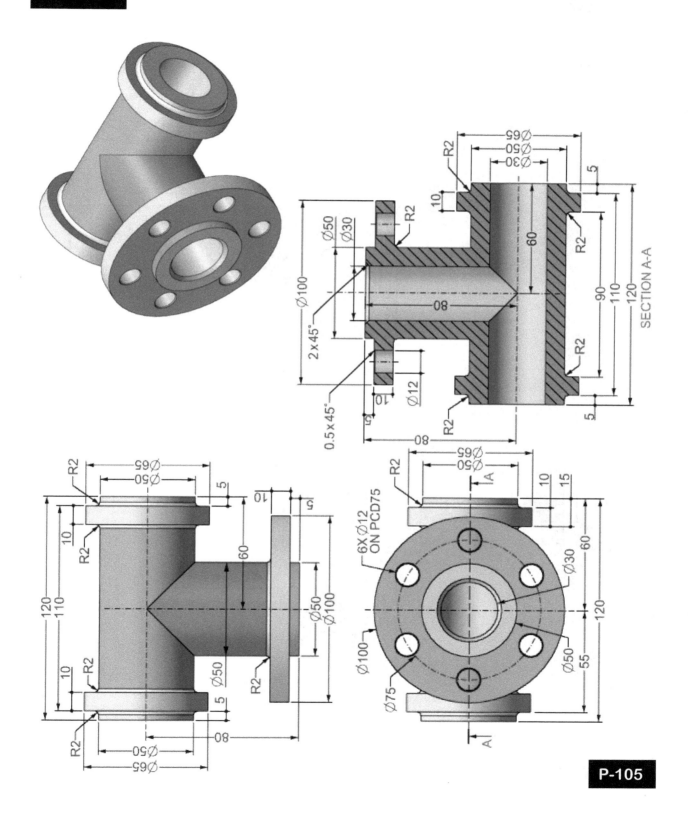

SECTION A-A

6X Ø12
ON PCD75

P-105

EX-200

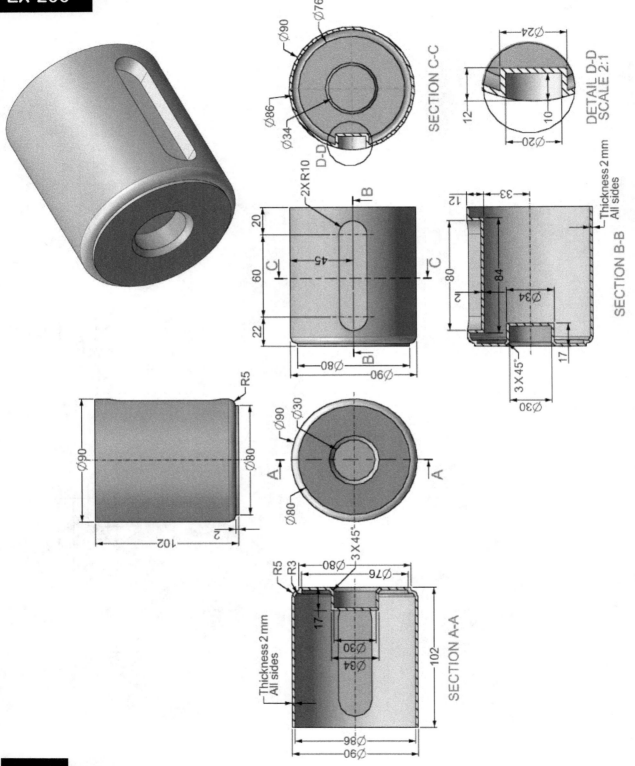

SECTION C-C

DETAIL D-D
SCALE 2:1

Ø90
Ø76
Ø86
Ø34
D-D

Ø24
12
10
Ø20

2X R10
B
20
C
45
60
C
22
B
Ø80
Ø90

12
33
80
84
Ø34
2
3 X 45°
17
Ø30
Thickness 2 mm
All sides

SECTION B-B

R5
Ø90
Ø80
2
102

Ø90
Ø30
A
A
Ø80

R5
R3
3 X 45°
Ø80
Ø76
17
Ø30
Ø84
102
Thickness 2 mm
All sides
Ø98
Ø90

SECTION A-A

P-106

Other useful books by CADIN360

1. 150 CAD Exercises

2. AutoCAD Exercises

3. CAD Exercises

4. 50+ SolidWorks Exercises

5. SolidWorks 200 Exercises

6. Autodesk Inventor Exercises

7. Catia Exercises

8. Siemens NX Exercises